Feat of Arms

or

THE SIEGE OF HADDINGTON

Gerald Urwin

Published in 2014 by FeedARead.com Publishing

Second Edition

A CIP catalogue record for this title is available from the British
Library.

CONTENTS.

Acknowledgements are due to :
Angus Mcbride of Osprey Publishing Ltd. for the colour plates of military
Scottish National Portrait Gallery for the portraits of Mary of Guise and Sir James Wilford.
Colin Will of Calder Wood Press for sound technical advice.
Haddington Library staff for unvarying, cheerful and prompt assistance.
Anna Dickie for the photos of cannon shot in the walls of St Mary's, Haddington.

Prologue 1

PROLOGUE.

In the summer of 1547, Sir William Grey, Governor of Berwick and Warden of the East Marches, came with his army and laid siege to Yester Castle, which lay three miles from Haddington. The besieged garrison comprising Scots and Spaniards offered a stout defence until Lord Grey brought up the great cannons. They soon made a substantial breach in the Castle wall, upon which the garrison sought mercy. This was granted save for one man who had reviled the King's name in the most opprobrious terms. Most claimed the accused was one Newton, but he, in turn, accused one Hamilton. Therefore a duel between them was arranged to take place in the market square at Haddington. Grey and his army entered Haddington without any resistance being shown and straightaway set up the lists for the combat between the two accused to take place. They entered the lists in their doublets and hose, armed with sword, buckler and dagger. They drew their swords and commenced to swing at each other ferociously.

The mighty swords clashed in mid-air about the combatants heads, but, such was the fury of the man Hamilton's assault that his adversary, Newton, gave ground, nearly stumbled, but staggered backwards again to regain his footing. Hamilton was at him once more, sword sweeping downwards in an attempt to cleave him in two. Newton took the impact on his buckler, the shock of the blow sending him back again. Immediately the dagger in Hamilton's left hand swung in a vicious arc towards Newton's throat. He parried it with his sword, still reeling backwards. Again Hamilton swung, again his opponent parried. They fought hard, furiously on Hamilton's part, in desperation Newton, to a nonstop accompaniment of roars and cheers from the assembled crowd of soldiers and citizens who lined the flimsy barricade of the lists. All the encouragement was for Hamilton, as he was the

innocent party in the eyes of the onlookers and falsely accused so far as they were concerned.

Still they fought on, with Newton barely able to save himself from Hamilton's devastating attack. Only by giving ground and retreating was he able to keep Hamilton at bay. But the end wall of the lists was getting closer, and he knew that if he was forced up against it then, by the laws of arms, he would concede the victory and be condemned to hang.

Still Hamilton swung and thrust, still Newton sweated and gave way. His eyes wide in panic, he stared as if fascinated at his opponent, repelling the blows instinctively. Adrenalin surged through his veins, sweat poured down his face, arms and body, his breathing grew faster and faster, strength seemed to ebb away from him -it was going to be the end, he knew it -then, above the unholy din a single female voice cried out triumphantly "Slay him, slay him, brave Hamilton".

The onslaught slackened momentarily as Hamilton acknowledged the voice with a smile and a slight turn of the head. Immediately Newton seized his chance and lunged forward with his dagger in the dreaded "arca" (commonly used in warfare to bring down a knight's horse) to slice the hamstring of his opponent's right leg. Hamilton gasped at the searing pain and stumbled forward on one knee. At once Newton was at him, thrusting, two handed now, his sword at Hamilton's throat. The point entered below the Adam's apple and emerged at the back of the head. A horrific gurgling broke from the stricken man. The crowd looked on horror-struck as Newton tugged his sword free, then plunged it into the already dead man's chest.

The crowd surged forward, outraged at the outcome. Hands stretched out for Newton to seek their own revenge.

"Hold, hold I pray thee" he cried. "I crave the laws of arms, your Excellency" looking anxiously at the stern faced nobleman, sitting astride a huge, gray charger and flanked by heralds and

men-at-arms.

Sir William Grey, for so it was, nodded. "Indeed you may, sire. Such was the agreement before you entered the lists. Give him this coat and chain". So saying he slipped off his own coat and chain and handed them to an attending herald.

Newton accepted the gifts, hurriedly mounted his horse which had been led to him and rode off.

Grey gave a curt nod to three knights-at-arms standing nearby who promptly mounted their own horses and gave chase to the victor of the duel. Sir William turned to those knights surrounding him.

"And now, gentlemen, let us to save Haddington from the French."

Chapter 1

CONFRONTATION.

Edward Seymour, Earl of Hertford, Duke of Somerset and Lord Protector, had modelled himself too much on his late monarch, Henry VIII, to consider a change of approach to the ever-present problem of Scotland and the Scots. There was to be no let up in forcing the Scots to join in a union with England and bring to an end centuries of struggle and warfare.

There were several aspects to his character which, although seemingly contradictory, nevertheless showed him to be a strong likeness to Henry. He was a petty tyrant who demanded unquestioning obedience from others. Highly intelligent he also showed surprisingly poor judgment in political matters. He could be extremely bad tempered but was not bloodthirsty in the way of many tyrants. He was a bully who shouted and blustered but never insisted on cruel punishment. He was prone to treat the Council of England as a rubber stamp ; he called it to session infrequently, harangued it when it did assemble and peremptorily dismissed members who disagreed with him. He appeared totally unable to recognise good advice, let alone act on it. Instead he was more likely to gamble on an outcome.

At waging war, however, he was brilliant, at least until the later stages of his Scottish campaign. His personal military experience was second to none. He was Commander in the North in 1542, acting as Warden of the Scottish Marches. In 1544 and 1545 he invaded Scotland successfully, while still fi nding time to race southwards and cross to France in order to capture Boulogne in January 1545. In June 1546 he concluded a peace treaty with the French and returned to

England, becoming Protector to the young Prince Edward when Henry died in January 1547.

Scotland, though, still remained as an unresolved problem. Despite a disastrous defeat at Pinkie on the 10th of September, 1547, most Scots remained resolute in their decision that there would be no Union, especially one brought about as a result of a marriage between the two wards, Edward and Mary.

A change of strategy, especially military strategy, was called for and Somerset was up to the task. He determined to defeat the Scots in effecting a permanent conquest of the country by building a series of fortified strongholds which would house full-time garrisons. He based his strategy on his knowledge of a technical development in the building of such strongholds and forts which was both quick and cheap. It was called the "Trace Italienne" and featured earth walls which were fifty to sixty feet thick, plus a diamond shaped bastion which afforded cover from all sides. He had also benefited from the experience of the previous campaign, culminating in a glorious victory at Pinkie, in which his army of 15,000, including mercenaries, had used moveable fi eld artillery and hand held guns to great effect. They had also been shadowed by a large fleet in the Forth, which had carried food for the army, munitions and supplies, thus relieving the need to provide a costly and vulnerable baggage train. The fl eet as well, of course, gave overwhelming fi re support and proved a key factor in the eventual outcome. All of these lessons had been well learned and were to be repeated in the forthcoming campaign.

HADDINGTON.

Haddington was chosen as a logical site for a stronghold.

Confrontation 7

It lay sixteen miles from the capital, Edinburgh, on the main route between England and Scotland, but not too far that it could not be reached quickly from the main English garrison at Berwick. It was also only a matter of fi ve miles or so from the Forth, so supplies could be landed nearby.

Its strategic importance was well known -"Most men think kepyng Haddyngton, ye wyne Skotland", as was reported to Somerset by Palmer, his engineer in the fi eld on June 30th, 1548. Somerset had determined on Haddington to be so massively fortified as to make it immune to any attack, a continuous presence among the Scots, designed to convince them that it was useless to resist any longer.

SIR WILLIAM GREY.

His commander in the field was Sir William Grey, 13th Baron de Wilton. A career soldier, he had behaved with great distinction at the siege of Chatillon in France, where he served from 1544 to 1546. From then until he died in December 1562, he was continually on call in most of the war arenas where English forces were involved. He was acknowledged as "one of the generals of the age" despite his oft repeated plea to be allowed to return home to a quiet rural existence in Hertfordshire. As Field Marshall and Captain-General of Horse he joined the invasion of Scotland and took part in the Battle of Pinkie where he was severely wounded in the mouth by a pike thrust which "clave one of his teeth, struck him through the tongue and three fingers deep into the roof of his mouth, yet, notwithstanding, he pursued out the chase wherein, what with the abundance of blood, heat of the weather, dust of the press, he had surely been suffocated had not the Duke of Northumberland alighted and lifted a firkin of ale to his head as they passed

through the Scottish camp".

He was knighted on the 29th of September, 1547, by Somerset at Berwick and created the Governor of Berwick and Warden of the East Marches. The following year, in January, he led a force of mercenaries and attacked Buccleuch and Branxholm. Then, with a much larger force, he captured and garrisoned Hailes, Herdmanston, Yester and Waughton before entering Haddington on the 18th of April, 1548.

ARRAN.

The opposing forces, gathering at Edinburgh to meet him, were led by James Hamilton, 2nd Earl of Arran, Regent of Scotland, who had succeeded his father, James, 1st Earl of Arran, in 1529 and, following the death of James V in 1542, became Regent during the minority of Queen Mary. As great grandson of James II he was also heir-presumptive to the throne. Thus the two leading combatants in the Anglo-Scottish struggle were each acting Commanders-in-Chief on behalf of two infant future monarchs. There the similarity ended, for their characters differed enormously. Arran was not a conventionally impressive man. He vacillated on important issues, was too easily persuaded by whatever argument he was listening to at the time, he acted foolishly and petulantly and suffered from bullying to which he was susceptible. For long periods he did nothing, despite pressure from those around him, which frequently reduced him to tears. When threatened he always conceded, taking a line of least resistance. He at all times looked out for himself and his family and was greedy when tempted. At Pinkie, when he had a God-given opportunity to triumph on the battlefield, he fled when a stronger leader would have taken

Confrontation 9

over at the moment of crisis, so losing a wonderful chance of immortality. Very few of his contemporaries could fi nd anything good to say about him.

Nevertheless he was the epitome of a born survivor. He held on to the post of Regent for twelve years, despite the machinations of powerful enemies within and outwith Scotland. In 1544 there were revolts in several areas of the realm which he put down. Henry VIII could never get the better of him, and, even after the disaster at Pinkie, he still clung to his position tenaciously. Internally his two greatest enemies were Cardinal Beaton and Mary of Guise. The former was eventually overcome and the latter was forced to wait before she could wrest the reins of state control from him.

In 1543 he had suggested the possibility of Union with

England but was never entirely serious in following it through to a conclusion. Rather it was as if he was trying to gain time to make his own position stronger. His actions subsequently gave the lie to any thought of allowing a marriage between Mary and Edward - he would decide who was to succeed. Rather than submit to Somerset's arguments, he preferred to allow the French to land in Scotland and take up the conflict as allies against the English, taking an enormous risk that a Catholic nation, France, would be preferred by the Scots to domination by the English.

Although he was very short of resources, both financial and political, he did possess powers which he was able to use to strengthen his position. As governor he could issue pardons, call Parliament to Session, raise armies and grant both title and land. He applied himself diligently to these functions to gain allies, but many Scots continued to hold

10 Confrontation

him in contempt ; indeed, on one notorious occasion, he was forced to take shelter in the Cathedral of St Giles in Edinburgh while attending a christening for "... the wyffes war lyke to have stoned hym to death".

D'ESSÉ

Commander of the French forces in Scotland between 1548 to 1550 was Andre de Montalambert, Sieur d'Essé, aged 65 and already known to the English opposing him who regarded him with considerable apprehension, having seen him in action at the sieges of Landrécy and Boulogne. De Beaugué, who served in the French army during the campaign in Scotland, regarded d'Essé with a devout hero worship, saying "...... men of the character of M.d'Essé are blest with this singular pre-eminency ; they have the same presence of mind, the same air and countenance in all the vicissitudes of fortune ; they never descend to irresolution or fear ; but, by the readiness of their own courage they keep up that of their followers in the midst of danger". In other words, like all good leaders, d'Esse led by example.

His ability to motivate those beneath him was shown by this short speech he made as the French force was about leave Edinburgh and move to Haddington.

"Though you had never before tried the English, yet I doubt not, brave soldiers, that the weakest among you would dare singly to encounter the stoutest man of that country this day in being. Tis certain, that had not honour and virtue held the fi rst rank in your breasts, you had not so cheerfully exposed your lives, nor come so willingly to a place like this, where reputation can be acquired and maintained by no other way, but that of doing well. In my opinion, there are very few or

Confrontation 11

none here, who have not only resisted the boasted force, but have several times humbled and reduced to reason this very enemy. And now since tis your happiness to have by you so very many brave men, at once the witnesses of your valour, and the guarantees of your victory, who can doubt but that we shall fi rst trod down, then thrust out by the shoulders, our enemy from this Kingdom ? For my own part, I resolve in this armour, both on foot and on horseback, to show you the path which leads to Glory : and I hope that this very arm, so often and so honourably dipped in English blood, shall yet again be felt by them not at all weakened, or short of what it has been. Believe me comrades, my heart and hands are the same as they were, and you'll infinitely more oblige me by imitating my deeds than by crediting my words".

D'Essé kept his soldiers occupied at all times, being conscious that idleness bred discontent, especially in a foreign land. Few of them grumbled, because to do so was to fall behind when the rest were seeking loot and plunder. Food and supplies of all types were not as available as would have been preferable, so D'Essé made his men forage everywhere, to the point that the land was laid waste.

His troops came from all parts of France, especially Brittany and Gascony, serving under such as Francois de Coligny, Sieur d'Andelot, commanding the foot, Francois d'Etauges commanding 1000 cavalry and Dunoon commanding the

artillery, by now an established feature of the battlefield.
Mercenaries were much in evidence, including a force of
Italians under Pietro Strozzi and Germans under Jean Philip
de Salm, Count Rhinegrave. The whole army eventually
landed in Leith on June 17th, 1548. D'Essé wasted no time
but gathered the provisions the Scots had ready and marched
12 Confrontation
to Haddington in late June.

MARY OF GUISE.

The Scots-French alliance, the cornerstone of Scots foreign
policy, was considerably strengthened by the person of
Mary of Guise-Lorraine, Duchess of Longueville who was
also Queen Dowager of Scotland. The widow of James V
of Scotland, she was also the mother of the infant Mary,
heiress to the throne, whose destiny and husband were the
cause of the intense struggle which was about to take place
in the Scottish lowlands.
Mary of Guise was the daughter of the Duc of Guise and
was born on the 22nd of November, 1515 at Bar-le-Duc.
Her picture, which hangs in the Scottish National Portrait
Gallery, Edinburgh, was reputedly painted by Corneille de
Lyon, and shows a fresh faced lady with dark blue eyes and
a hint of auburn hair, who is surprisingly plainly dressed
in a robe with a square-necked bodice and a black, closefitting
hood. At the Court of Henry II of France, she was
regarded as a beauty. In August 1534 she married Louis of
Orleans and gave birth in October 1535 to Francis, a son.
Her husband died in June 1538, but, although pursued by
Henry VIII of England, she chose instead to wed James V of
Scotland, thus uniting the two kingdoms further. She landed
at Crail, in the Kingdom of Fife on June 11th, 1539. Her
daughter, who was to become Mary, Queen of Scots, was
born at Linlithgow Palace on December 2nd, 1542. Two
weeks later, James himself died, paving the way for Arran's
Regency which was approved by the Scots Parliament on
12th March, 1543. At the same time Henry's offer to marry
Edward to Mary was accepted by Parliament and supported

by Mary of Guise.
But Cardinal Beaton was having none of it. Aware of the
level of public feeling which was strongly opposed to the
match, he carried both mother and daughter to Stirling. In
September, 1543 Arran performed another volte-face, was
reconciled with Beaton and rejected the English proposal.
On 6th October, the French ambassador De La Brosse
offered assistance and a military alliance to stand against
England. On the 3rd December, 1543 the Scots Parliament
accepted. In a rage, Henry declared war. Arran's army
was decisively beaten at Pinkie Cleugh, so Mary raised
a new army to halt English progress. She despatched her
daughter to Inchmahome Island, in the Lake of Menteith,
for safekeeping.

On the 8th February, 1548, a Convention at Stirling of
Scottish nobles agreed to the marriage of the child Mary and
the French Dauphin. She was to be sent at once to France.
Her mother, though, was still a Scottish Dowager-Queen and
expected to stay in Scotland, even though poverty dogged
her steps, albeit in relation to various nobles, as, indeed,
was the case with Arran himself. She borrowed money
from the Countess of Montrose and others and needed to
show ingenuity and courage to protect her position. She
accomplished this by gathering allies around her, including
those to whom she was in debt. Although still an attractive
woman, she was by no means empty headed. The way in
which she manoeuvred Arran, Beaton and others showed
great guile and perception. She was no fool and would
not tolerate any attempt to undermine her position. When
she perceived a seeming indifference among the Scots in
Edinburgh to the French soldiery at Haddington, she rode

through the city and addressed the local citizenry.

"Is it thus, my friends, that you second the French ? Is this
the example you give them ? Had not my own eyes informed
me of this your forgetfulness of honour and duty, I should

never have been prevailed upon to believe it. I ever thought,
and am still willing to entertain the same sentiments, that no
nation under the sun can vye with your inbred and unequalled
gallantry ; for after all, it may be, and I flatter myself tis
so, that you come not hither to avoid fi ghting. Forbid it, O
heavens ! But to furnish yourselves with arms and horses,
to fi ght with the greater advantage. Persuaded then, that
tis beneath the grandeur of Scottish souls to deserve a just
reproach, I give you to know, that within the short space of
two days, we shall have a battle at Haddington ; I know you
could never forgive yourselves the unpardonable omission,
if through your own negligence or inaction, you should
miss of the longed for opportunity you now have in your
hands, to repay the injuries received from this very enemy ;
injuries, no less, than the ransacking your goods, the laying
waste your inheritances, and the bringing death to those
parents that gave you life, and to those friends that made
life desirable to you".
The response was immediate and the Scots fl ocked to join
their French allies.
She had not finished with her exhortations for it was made
known to her that there were large numbers of French troops
still in Edinburgh. She made haste to confront them.
"I am very much surprised that you who have betaken
yourselves to arms, and have already made such forward
advances on the road to honour, should not be more afraid of
being, through your own fault, deprived of that reputation,

yourselves and all good men have placed in the foremost
rank of blessing. Five or six thousand English are at hand,
with a desire to beat us from before Haddington, but care
is already taken, God willing, to frustrate their attempt. I
cannot doubt but that you seek honour, merely for honour's
sake, as believing it a full return and compensation for all
the valour you can express ; and therefore should be sorry,
if you shared not in the assured glory that waits your fellow
soldiers in the camp. For the truth is these brave men are

sufficiently numerous to have certain victory without your additional assistance ; but then the English shall only feel the weight of their arms, and the universe shall loudly proclaim your infamy. However, do as you please. I assure myself you will not cannot do amiss."

Her speech had the desired effect. Within the hour there was not one soldier to be seen in the city. She did not confi ne herself to condemnation only ; she could be fair and give praise when it was justified. She addressed the French officers after an action before Haddington in these words : "I ever esteemed you but I should prove ungrateful if I could fail to love every one of you, after the signal service you have done me. Assure yourselves, nothing in my power shall be wanting to testify the value I set upon your merits : and since the state of this Kingdom and my service depends on you, tis but reasonable that I should see you rewarded. I have ordered some presents for you ; receive them as an earnest of my further liberalities. I hope to be, one day, in a condition to make you acknowledge that the rewards of victory are greater than the hazards of war".

It is hardly surprising to learn that she was very quickly a favourite with the Allied forces before Haddington. De

16 Confrontation

Beaugué claimed "...... she was absolute mistress of the hearts and hands of the French, and had charmed them into a forwardness to do anything for her service. On the other hand, her clemency, justice, liberality, prudence and holiness of life, were respected by all the better sort of the Queen her daughter's subjects".

These, then, were the principal protagonists on the eve of the armed struggle for Haddington, with a greater prize waiting in the future.

15

Edward Seymour, Duke of Somerset. (1506 –1552)

Sir James Wilford

Mary of Guise-Lorraine

James Hamilton, Second Earl of Arran

ANDRÉ DE MONTALEMBERT,
Comte d'Essé, Lieutenant Général pour le
Roi, Commandant ses Armées en Ecosse. Gouver-
neur de Teroane. Mort sur la Breche de cette ville le 12.
1553.

Chapter 2

FORTIFICATION.

Somerset's strategy to build a series of fortresses or
strongholds in the lands leading to Edinburgh did not
envisage stone-built castles. For one thing this would have
been too long and costly a project to carry out, and it is
extremely doubtful if it would ever have been allowed to be
completed by the Scots and their French allies. Rather did
Somerset have in mind fortifications, which could be quickly
and cheaply erected using readily available materials, based
on the "Trace Italienne" (the Italian Plan) which he had
learned about in the course of his own military adventures.

SIR THOMAS PALMER.

His engineer in-chief was to be Sir Thomas Palmer,
experienced in this line of work and with a reputation for
unbounded courage. A military careerist he had also been
in attendance as a gentleman usher to Henry VIII at the
flamboyant "Field of the Cloth of Gold" in 1520. From there
he had progressed from a position as an "overseer of petty
customs" and surveyor of the lordship of Henley-in -Arden
to joining the expedition of 1523 where he had served with
distinction. On the 10th of November 1532 he was knighted
at Calais and was appointed the Knight Porter of Calais the
following year. In 1547 he joined the march northwards and
showed himself to be a dauntless fighter in combat against
the Scots. Nevertheless it was as a planner and engineer
that his true skill was about to manifest itself. Despite his
appointment he continued to loathe and detest Somerset.
On April 18th 1548, Grey entered Haddington with 2000
foot and 500 horse, and the work started in earnest and went
24 Fortification
on until the besieging forces arrived in late June. When
completed the fortification was the most scientific military
work of its class hitherto constructed in Scotland, if not the
whole of Britain.
Haddington is located in the middle of a low plain with

21

no rising ground or hills which could overlook it. The Garleton Hills were more than a cannon shot distant and the Lammermuirs even more. The stronghold, when built, took the form of an enormous low and squat quadrangular curtain wall, wholly constructed of earth and turf some fifty feet thick, materials which were, of course, readily to hand in a rich, agricultural landscape. Timbers, including faggots, rods and heather included in the earthworks were cut in the woods adjacent to the town. There was a strong bastion at each corner. A bastion was a strongly fortified outwork, built in the shape of a five-pointed star, which, although attached to the main works, projected outwards from it. Sunk into the earth of the bastions were "flankers" i.e. gun mounts. Any invader engaged in an assault on the main "wall" would be fired on from these bastions regardless of whatever angle of approach he took. Outside the quadrangle was a large, flat-bottomed ditch, some thirty feet across and twelve feet deep. On top was a spacious rampart, with "good and safe breastworks", which could be manned by bowmen, arquebusiers etc.. Behind was another ditch, bordered by a curtain wall of earth and four turrets which surrounded and protected a "donjon" or keep, itself providing a final refuge to the garrison and used as a headquarters and an arsenal during the siege. As such it took the form of a high, square tower with very thick walls placed in the centre of the fortifications, and not attached to any

Fortification 25

other. In normal circumstances it contained a Great Hall and a prison (dungeon). Between the curtain and the ditch were casemates (chambers in the thickness of the wall, provided with embrasures for defence.) As well as these main features, there were included several more earthworks, platforms and "ravelins" (a two-sided outwork built to protrude from the main curtain.) On these were sited several cannon, "mostly of a middle size", (probably culverins.) Altogether, when finished, it was "..........one of the finest and strongest after Turin." (Bertville.)

Palmer was well pleased. "The Haddyngtons hathe doon ondres in their fortefycacions, nothing left unperfected" he wrote to Somerset on June 30th. It was a timely letter for the same day the French arrived and immediately set to besieging the town. These wonderful fortifications, however, have left no trace. Being precise as to their exact location is not easy but there are some clues.

Various commentators and correspondents agree that the original town buildings were left standing and intact for the most part, at least at the beginning of the siege. "Within the enclosure remained the substance of all the town and fair houses" says one. Palmer himself wrote "..........the captain and his garrison......place themselves in cabonettes on the ramparts, lodging in the town only at need" and "I am sure that I know the town as well as they do......."It was also noted "..........there was a clearance of buildings on the bank of the river". It was also noted that "The convent of Franciscan Friars was included in the works". Another comments "..........town houses were incorporated into the curtain walls". Evidently the river Tyne bordered one wall of the quadrangle. From these clues a picture starts to
26 Fortification
emerge.

If one side of the quadrangle consisted of town houses, then , given Haddington's peculiar isosceles triangle shape, it must have been either the north side or the south side of the town, which we know nowadays as Market Street or the High Street. Haddington has always, so far as is known, been of an elongated triangular shape, with the short side nearest to the river. If this short side was removed, as shown, then the choice of curtain wall lies between the other two. Furthermore, if the entire structure was square, as quoted in the "Inventory of Monuments in East Lothian", and not merely quadrangular, then it follows that the other three sides were of the same length as the side comprising town buildings. Therefore, only two options are available -either the "square" ran northwards of the High Street or it ran southwards of Market Street. The length of a"side" is further confi rmed by the discovery of a trench by workmen digging in Market Street in the nineteenth century, which pinpoints one of the walls which Palmer's men raised so long ago. The other information given helps to make the choice more assured. The river, we are told, bordered the town, and the Franciscan Friary was included within the walls. If the walls ran northwards, then a square shape would show the river Tyne to flow through the town, and not alongside as was quoted. However, if the square ran southwards from Market clues, then all the information given, or Clues, is shown to fi t, i.e. the Friary is inside the walls, the river runs along the border with the eastern wall, all of the town buildings are include within the walls, and, crucially, St Mary's Church is within range of the town cannon, "........for our ordnance beats through the steeple at every shot........."

Fortification 27

CONDITIONS IN HADDINGTON.

Life within the town was to prove very diffi cult, but, unfortunately, not enough information has been left to us to know exactly how the garrison and townsfolk coped with the stringencies of the situation in which they found themselves. How, for instance, did they dispose of corpses ? It would have proved to be too great a health hazard to bury them within the walls, so, presumably they were taken away in the two or three carts which made the hazardous journey to Dunbar on a quite regular basis. The stabling of the horses must also have presented a problem to Wilford, the town commandant. At the start of the siege he had at least 500 to deal with ; on June 30th Grey was writing to Somerset "........ there are not past 120 left of the 400 I placed there. Some fl ed to the West Border for whom I wrote to the Warden, others keep among the "assured" Scots. John Carr drove some back, the Laird of Langton took two, and Colbie, a captain at Roxburgh, one........" By the 24th of July, Brende, a captain based at Berwick, was writing to Somerset to inform him "........our horses are sore diminished.....of 300

demilances but 36 fi t for service ; of 450 new light horse,
not 100 available........"

The picture presented suggests a high death rate for horses
inside the walls, which is understandable given the amount
of cannon fi re they had to endure.

MILITARISATION.

On one thing were both Fulwell, the English commentator,
and De Beaugué, who actually served in the French force
at Haddington, agreed - the besieged garrison deserved
full praise for their courage and resilience. Although
Fulwell's enthusiasm in praise of his fellow countrymen
is understandable, that of De Beaugué is a surprise, since
especially in other sections of his "History of the Campagnes,
1548 and 1549, he is not at all enamoured of the English " a
People always tainted with that heresy ...... which imposes
upon them a false belief of their merit, beyond that of all
the nations of the world...." Nevertheless, during the siege,
he commented that "............ for the most part were all
English.... had signalised their courage in several remarkable
exploits...........they were very brave men." Fulwell, of
course, had no problem in waxing enthusiastically about the
English troops- "Insomuch that the Frenchmen that were
there to the aid of the Scots say, unto this day, that there
are few good soldiers in England except those that were
at this siege of Haddington preferring the service that was
then there before any other that ever they knew or heard
of......."

THE ENGLISH FORCE.

One or two commentators on the siege assert that the majority
of those forces involved were mercenaries, but, although
"soldiers of fortune" were present on either side, a muster
of troops prepared by Brende at Berwick shows that the foot
soldiers Grey had in Scotland were predominantly English.
It is true they were supported by German "landsknecht"
troops, some Albanians (from many of the Balkan states),

Chapter 3

a few Spaniards and some Italians. Arquebusiers were invariably from overseas, since Henry VIII had banned the new-fangled "fi re machine" two years previously in favour of the longbow, but the mounted horse soldiery were almost entirely English. Landsknecht were pikemen, originally Swiss but since adopted by several other European nations, especially the Germans, following their outstanding success in Italy etc., as a professional hired force. They favoured a long Morris (Moorish) pike, some sixteen to eighteen feet long. The English pike was shorter in length. Flodden had been won by use of the "bill" but Henry was shrewd enough to realise that battles against the French would require a much longer weapon.

Grey brought 500 horse to Haddington. Some men-at-arms still wore heavy plate armour and needed a powerful shire horse to carry them, but they were the exception. Most of the horse present at Haddington were "demilances", with lighter armour worn over the arms, upper body and thighs. They carried a spear and sword by their side. The horse they rode was much speedier than the "shire". It was the horse that ventured forth most often, mainly to secure the convoys of supplies from Dunbar, but also to harass the enemy when the opportunity presented itself. Some of the arquebusiers, or "hackbutters" as the English called them, were also mounted. The " hackbut", from the German "hackenbusche", threw a 1 oz. pellet. Brende, the Berwick-based captain, advised Somerset on the 7th of July, 1548, that "..............110 in Wyndham's band, 150 in Gamboa's under Petro Negro, and 100 in Bagshot's band, all mounted hackbutters with a bag of gunpowder and a roll of match were waiting at Linton" (now East Linton). Certainly

Wyndham's men and Bagshot's played leading roles in the siege. Evidence of their handiwork can still be seen on the walls of St Mary's facing towards Haddington, which are pitted with holes caused by the defenders' fi re.

The day of the longbow, however, was not done with. Bowmen certainly played their part in the defence of the town. Grey reported to Somerset on the 30th of June, 1548, the first day of the siege, "...the French horse was driven off ....many of their horses carried away arrows in them". For the foot soldiers therefore, the enemy was to be repelled with arrow, shot and pike. The use of the pike was the most problematical, because to stretch down from the parapet in order to lunge at an attacker was to attract a response which involved grabbing the pike, with the very possible result that the defender could be dislodged and dragged down to the ground, there to be slaughtered at leisure. It is probable that pikemen were kept back to repel intruders and to serve as escorts when a sortie was made from the stronghold. Although hand-to-hand combat took place at the curtain wall, it was not a regular occurrence. Missile projection was the order of the day.

The most useful and frequent missile was provided by the middle range cannon which Grey brought to Haddington. The siting of the cannon batteries was invariably determined by the enemy ; wherever he attacked, especially with his own cannon, then the defenders' cannon were brought to bear on them, usually from bulwarks opposite. The most heavily engaged bulwarks, throughout the siege, were those of Wyndham and Bowes. Wyndham's battery was located on the south side, nearest to the heaviest concentration of French troops at Clerkington. Bowes was to the north,

facing a French battery " ....three pieces of artillery on the crag towards Aberlady."

D'Essé himself was foolish enough to come within range of Wyndham's battery on the 3rd July 1548, in order that he might inspect a possible breach in the curtain wall. There were some 9 or 10 shots fi red at his party which killed at least four of them and caused the French commander to retire swiftly to his camp. However, Wilford, the garrison commandant, was continually running short of powder and shot, which caused his cannon to fall silent at times. Fortunately supplies always arrived somehow because the besiegers never entirely succeeded in surrounding the town entirely, nor in blocking the supply routes from Dunbar and Berwick.

Armour was worn mainly by the gentry ; in this case that meant the mounted horse, mostly "demilances", wearing three-quarter armour covering the body and sometimes, but not invariably, a "burgonet" or helmet. The humble foot soldier wore a canvas "jack" (hence jacket) lined with metal plates covered by cloth. Some of the lucky ones may have worn a breast and back plate made of "Almain rivet". All wore a white shirt with a red cross on the front.

Such were the forces on the English side. The age of the regiment was still over a hundred years away. A feudal system still operated in England whereby the lord of the manor was required by the King to supply a number (usually a hundred) of men to serve in the campaign of the moment. in return for a strip of land, on which could be grown crops, the men who lived on the land were required to serve their lord and master when needed. Thus we fi nd that Wyndham, Taylor, Booth, Ashby and the rest each had 100 men under

his command. Some lords had 200.

THE ASSURED SCOTS.

They were not entirely without friends in Scotland. Henry VIII had enlisted the promises of several Scots nobles, captured at Solway Moss in 1542, including William Cunningham, Earl of Glencairn, Gilbert Kennedy, Earl of Cassillis, Robert Maxwell, Malcolm Fleming, Patrick Gray and Hugh Somerville. These men controlled enormous areas of land south of the Clyde-Forth line. Archibald, Earl of Angus and Sir George Douglas of Pittendriech, kept him well informed of what was happening at the Scottish Parliament by use of spies. These spies moved between both camps and sometimes Edinburgh, for instance "...........the spy says they have promised to deliver it (i.e. Haddington) to the French King by Tuesday next" and "......one of our most assured spies..... that Pedro Strose was shot through the thigh by an arquebus and was carried in a cart by his men, in crimson and white velvet..." and also "........... we hear by one that was at the camp at four o'clock this morning." The Earl and Sir George also promised to do their best to promote the marriage of Edward and Mary, and signed articles which bound them to the King's service. At the time of the Haddington siege many other Scots gentry joined the cause, including Brynston, Langton, Cesford, Fernihurst, Huntly, Leverton, Colston, Hugh Douglas of Longniddry, Wittingham, Ruthen, Melvin and Mellerstain. The Earls Athol , Crawford, Marshall, Sutherland, Errol and Rothes also played their part. Pressure was put on them to demonstrate, in a practical way, that they intended to keep their word. Brende, writing from Berwick on July

26th, 1548, was on their tail "............Cesford, Ferniherst and Hundelee constant in proffers of service. The rest either enemies or doubtful friends, for neither Leveston, Colston, Hugh Douglas of Longniddry, Wytingham nor any other of Lothian have showed either good will or service". Patrick, Lord Gray wrote to Somerset on August 28th, 1548 to advise him "I have spoken with the Earls of Athol, Crawford, Marshall, Sutherland, Rothes and Errol and other gentlemen who are of good mind to the King's godly purpose.............. I would your Grace send some wise man to get their full minds, and to give them some money after their desserts." Locally, the garrison was well served, being supplied with food by several of the nearby lairds. It was a fact of life which irritated the French commandant, who made his feelings known to Arran. Towards the second half of the siege, there was a "tightening up", with the local lairds being threatened until they desisted in their efforts to assist the English garrison. This, coupled with the general laying waste of the surrounding countryside, made life even more diffi cult for Wilford (and later Acroft) and his men.

At the conclusion of the campaign, a total of 955 Scots were found guilty of having donned the mantle of the "assured" Scots, mainly in the Borders. They were, for the most part, dealt with comparatively leniently, being fi ned and then forgiven.

THE FRENCH FORCE.

It seems probable that D'Essé, landing at Leith in June, 1548 with his 6,000 men, did not have a prolonged investiture of Haddington in mind. His orders were to evict the English from all of Scotland, which included other places such

as Broughty Castle near Dundee, Dunbar and the Border strongholds, not just Haddington. He opted to attack Haddington first, hoping for a swift victory before turning his attention to the others. When this proved beyond him, he changed his plan to one of containment while directing his forces elsewhere. He could always ask the Scots to "hold the Fort" pending reinforcements.

His army was divided into two parts ; the one consisting of Germans under the command of Count Rhinegrave, and the other a French force under the dashing d'Andelot. The composition of his army refl cted to a large extent that of the enemy, including a large number of German and Swiss landsknecht, Italians and Spaniards. His foot soldiers were mainly pikemen, the pike still being the preferred choice of European armies of the day. His cavalry consisted mainly of demilances although there were also some light horse and men-at-arms on heavy shire horses. Arquebusiers featured heavily but there were also archers and interestingly even crossbowmen. De Beaugué noted "...a soldier of Gascony bended his crossbow and from there shot twice in upon the enemy..."

Cannon also featured prominently ; D'Essé had both middle and heavy guns available. When it became obvious that the siege was likely to be prolonged, he withdrew all cannon, save six, to Edinburgh. The ones that remained were probably culverins. A culverin was a long barrelled, long range gun midway between a large cannon and a falconet. Its name was derived from the old French "coulevrine" meaning a snake. A full culverin fi red a sixteen pound shot. Surprisingly there were no mortars among the ordnance, even though D'Essé must have seen them in effective action

at the siege of Boulogne in 1544, where Henry VIII had fi fty of them pounding away. Their effect on a beleaguered garrison inside the earth walls of Haddington, which itself was a very much smaller target area than Boulogne, would surely have been quite devastating. It is quite likely that D'Essé would have achieved his primary aim and thus have been able to stick to his original plan. Fortunately for Wilford and his men mortars were not used during the siege - an oversight which, with the benefit of hindsight, seems incredible.

The Scots allies in the field were an entirely different proposition to either the French or the English forces. They were not a regular army, being composed of irregular, ad hoc troops. Once the battle was over they were more than likely to go home and resume their normal existence. As De Beaugué explained "......Scots never take the field but when forced to arms by necessity.....carry all necessaries....make it their business to seek out the enemy with all expedition and fight with invincible courage. This done, and their victuals being consumed, they break up their camp and retire".

He also noted "............Scots from Orkney and the South assembled in great numbers in Edinburgh. They came to Haddington and stayed for eighteen to twenty days.......... charged the gates of Haddington.......they wore coats of mail, each with a large bow in his hand, and their quivers, swords and shields hand, as it were, in a sling. They were followed by several Highlanders and these last go almost naked : they have painted waistcoats and a sort of woollen covering variously coloured, and are armed as the rest with large bows, broadswords and targets.............advanced upon

five to six hundred that were posted between the port and
the barriers, but the noise of the artillery, with which they
had not been acquainted, soon quelled their courage. The
Highlanders shut their ears and threw themselves on their
bellies at each shot of the cannon". Many of the Scots,
who had seen many years of suffering at the hands of the
English, were only too keen to get their revenge when the
chance arose. At this time their actions shocked their more
humane and chivalrous French allies. On one occasion,
after the affair known as " Tuesday's Chase", he observed
"............Scots thronged the camp and beheld the naked
and mangled bodies of the English..............had the cruelty
to pull out the eyes of the dead...." Not long after, all the
Scots, except for some six hundred demilances of Arran and
Huntly, withdrew to their respective homes.

Preparations for the siege were commenced by D'Essé as
soon as his army arrived at Haddington on June 30th, 1548.
Brende, writing to Paget on July 2nd, says "Haddington is
now besieged and enclosed round about -they are making
trenches, and tomorrow I judge will plant their artillery".
Trenches were dug by the Germans "beyond the bridge
and trenching alongside the waterside to the mill that was
fortifi ed, but abandoned by our men as untenable". The
French "..........have brought 10,000 faggots....we think
to reinforce their battery trench, being so near the town".
On the 4th July, 1548, "........the French are now trenching
towards Holcroft's curtain to plant ordnance there". The
Scots were encamped at the nunnery to the north east and
the Highlanders contingent on a hill to the north.

It was now time for the bombardment to begin and for the
dreadful truth to dawn on D'Essé. For the most part the
bombardment produced little or no effect on the earthen
walls of the defences. As quickly as a breach appeared ,
those inside fi lled it in so that the wall was, in many cases,
stronger than before. Many of the shots sailed over the walls

and the whole town to land beyond. In one day the Scots
fi red 340 cannon shots without effecting any lasting damage
at all. Palmer had done his work well. The only success of
the bombardment came when the southwest bastion guns
were silenced, but, for some unknown reason, D'Essé let the
chance to invade slip by. Wilford carried on with his earthen
fortifi cations and, by the 22nd July, 1548, was claiming that
the town was five times stronger than before.

The weather played its part to dampen the spirits of the
attackers. De Beaugué complained "......the day was rainy
and the heavens were clouded by a thick mist to which
the Scots climate is very obnoxious". Later he was again
despondent "...........by reason of the continual rain".
Digging trenches in such weather was never going to lift
French morale.

The English, however, were never content to allow the
French preparations to go unchallenged. Sallies were made
regularly, both to attack those busy with the entrenching
and to gather supplies. Attacks on horseback were carried
out on the Scots pioneers who were digging a trench on the
left side of the Abbey port "...............and to cut out such
other fortifications as were thought fittest to shelter us from
the fire of the enemy...............the English made several
sallies...........M. Strozzi was dangerously wounded".
Later De Beaugué was reporting "............the English sallied
forth one night at eleven p.m. ....two hundred English
and Italian horse...........made a compass around the hill of
Aberlady. At the same time the Governor himself broke out

likewise upon the head of 400 English and Italian foot and 60
Scots peasants, with a view to sieze some barley...........".
D'Essé did not give up "...............caused expedite the work
of the trenches with that diligence that in two days time
they were advanced to the foot of the bulwark which we
attempted by sapping.......about eleven p.m. advanced the
" gabionados" and made loopholes for six guns...........and
thence, by break of day, we wakened those in Haddington

with a vengeance and battered at once the wall betwixt the port of Edinburgh and Tiberio's bulwark and the breastworks of the curtain............the curtain, being wonderfully thick and made of earth which deadened and drowned the balls, remained entire, notwithstanding our battery, neither did we any great harm to the wall............replaced the guns a hundred paces from the ditch............again discharged our guns a hundred times, yet all this was but noise, it did us no real good".

The final insult came when D'Etauges, sent to watch for the English supply route, was misled by a Scots spy ("the man with two heads") so that 200 English troops carrying powder, shot and other supplies were able to slip past 8000 Scots and Frenchmen in the mist "at a distance no greater than 200 paces".

1 - Billman
2 - Archer
3 - Footsoldier

1 - Border Horseman
2,3 - German Landsknechts

1-Pikeman
2-Demilance
3-Foot-soldier

1-German cavalryman
2-Arquebusier

Damage to the external wall of St Marys, caused by cannon and arquebus.

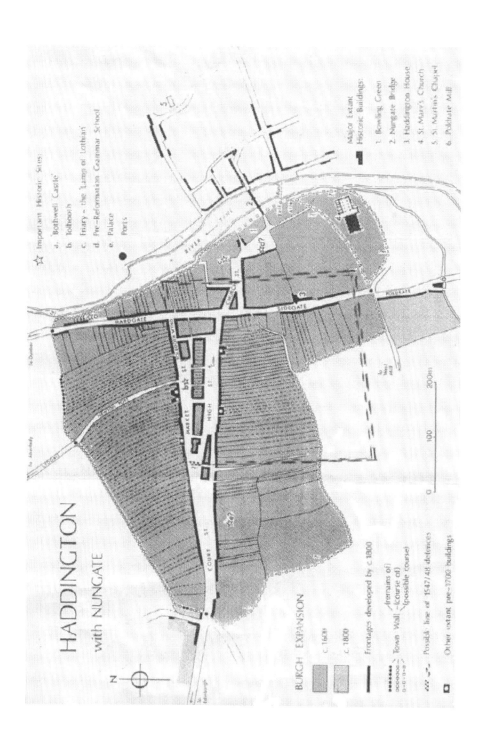

Map Of Haddington

40

Chapter 4
INTERACTION.

The siege of Haddington was reported at the time by De
Beaugué for the French. Later an English version of events
was penned by Ulpian Fulwell. The two versions differ in
their accounts, especially in relation to the numbers of dead,
wounded and taken prisoner, but agree substantially on the
more important actions. Both versions consider that the
most praise is due to their side and the available evidence
needs to be considered closely before an opinion as to what
actually happened can be formed.

It was a siege, insofar as the term is generally understood,
only occasionally. Continuous siege conditions, in which
the besieger does not allow any access from outside to the
besieged, occurred only on the odd occasion. Quite often
the besieger withdrew his forces, either in part or entirely ;
quite often supplies, including fresh troops, found their way
into Haddington despite the best efforts of the surrounding
forces. The garrison changed continuously, either because
of death, wounds, illness or simply fatigue, so that it is
almost impossible to know if any individual was present
throughout. Similarly, the Scots especially were forever
coming and going from the besiegers' camp, while French
activities in other parts meant that troops were often
despatched elsewhere. As far as the civilian population
of the town is concerned, it is diffi cult to imagine anyone
choosing to endure the noise and devastating effects of
continuous battle, nor the lack of food, for very long. It is
much more likely that they all stole away during the night
to a more secure area and environment.

The siege lasted for eighteen months, from April 18th, 1548

until October 1st, 1549. It was characterised by military
action on an almost daily basis once the French had arrived
in June until such time that they reverted to a strategy of

starvation by cutting off the supply routes, by bravery and chivalry on both sides, by examples of extreme cruelty by the besieging Scots, by hardship and endurance on the part of those confined within the walls of the besieged town, and by daily examples of foolishness and bravado.

It brought together English, Spaniards, Germans, Italians and Albanians on the defenders' side. Scots, French, Swiss, Italians, Spaniards and Germans were ranged against them. The English fought to pacify their old enemy the Scots, who, in turn, fought to defend their own country. The French fought both to defeat an old foe and to begin a promising alliance with their Scottish allies. The Germans, Italians and Albanians etc. fought for money.

COMMUNICATIONS AND ACTION.

Throughout, the main channel of communications for the besieged forces was via the north east port and thence to Dunbar and Berwick. Communication links with both Grey, waiting at Berwick, and Somerset in England, were restricted to routes via Lauderdale and Cockburnspath, although a third via Stenton was mooted but never attempted. Nevertheless messengers made their perilous path on horseback frequently enough. June 25th, 1548 saw the beginning of a fl urry of correspondence between the various English commanders, both inside and outwith the besieged burgh of Haddington. On this day Grey reported that the Scots were still not present in force and promised Wilford substantial support from both land and sea. The latter message was Interaction 49 cunningly designed to be deliberately intercepted so that the besiegers would be delayed into taking aggressive action. Grey reminded Somerset that 200 demilances and 300 light horse were promised to be despatched by Lord Shrewsbury on June 22nd, to be reinforced, furthermore, the following day by a further 1000 horse.

Meantime Grey sought support from Lord Wharton and Sir Thomas Dacres. He warned Wilford that the French intended to besiege him but that the English fleet would burn

the French fl eet together with all stores. He advised that
Courtpenny and a great band of German auxiliaries were
waiting to embark at Calais. Further support was coming
from the King's men-at-arms, plus 4000 horse, all headed
for Haddington. Andreas and his Albanians, together with
Philip Pini and his Italians had already left London, headed
north. Lord Shrewsbury, Lord Dacres etc...,were marching
north with 16000 men.

The following day he wrote again to Somerset to tell him
that the French, supported by the Scots, were en route for
Haddington, intending to set up several camps and batteries
of ordnance. He regretted that an insufficient number of
horse, ("many of the garrison horses already dead, and none
coming from Lord Wharton and only a few from the Bishop
of Durham and the Earl of Westmoreland") meant that he
was unable to harass the enemy as he would have wished.

On June 29th, Palmer advised Somerset that he had arrived
at Haddington at six a.m. and immediately set to work to
reinforce the walls surrounding the town. He ordered 200
loads of stakes and rods and various tools for quarrying. He
reported seeing many "horse" arriving at Haddington, plus
twenty demilances from Lord Shrewsbury. He did not think

the enemy had many horsemen, and were waiting for their
guns to be landed, probably at Aberlady, although he was
scornful of any threat to the besieged garrison.

A skirmish took place which was reported the next day by
Grey to Somerset. While ten horsemen from Haddington
waited for the captain of the Dunbar garrison, they saw the
young Laird of Waughton with a band of supporters. They
charged and captured the standard and standard bearer. The
rest ran away. On the key issue of the moment, he reported
that he had heard that the Scots were resolved to marry off
the young Mary to the French Dauphin. This information
was provided by Angus, George Douglas and several other
"assured" Scots noblemen. On hearing that 2000 sheep
and 100 head of cattle had been secured by Wilford over

and above what Grey had left, he sent Petro Negro and a hundred Spanish troops to augment the garrison. However, on seeing that the town was besieged, this force retired to Berwick. He regretted that there was no sign of Lord Dacre or Lord Wharton and their troops, despite his urgings.

He also reported an artillery duel between three cannon sited on the crags on the Aberlady road, and the battery at Bowes bulwark, plus the loss of some 280 light horse, some fl eeing west, some seeking refuge with the "assured" Scots. He promised to recapture some and make an example of at least two of them. Finally he reported the fi rst serious assault by the French horse and foot "coming no nearer the ditch that many of their horses carried away arrows in them". The assault was repeated "at break of day" but was driven off again "..........divers were left on the fi eld and many carried off across their horses, among them a French gentleman of estimation slain". He regretted that, since the enemy had

retired to their camp at seven a.m. and were still there at six p.m. "so the Spaniards might well enough have got into the town".

On the same day Palmer reported to Somerset that the fortifi cations were in good shape "nothing left unperfected". The garrison were so pleased with their work that 2000 of them, ensigns fl ying, "marched to the top of the hills in great triumph". Palmer was very bullish about the outcome of the siege, writing that "most men think, keeping Haddington, you win Scotland".

On July 2nd, 1548, Palmer and Holcroft jointly sent a despatch to Somerset advising of the enemy dispositions. The Germans had dug themselves a trench alongside the river next to the fortified mill which the English had abandoned as undefendable. The French and the Italians were based at Clerkington together with their ordnance. The rest were in camp on the other side of a hill towards Lethington.

Later in the day a second letter reported the French to have installed ten cannon on Lethington hill. They brought with

them 10,000 faggots, supposedly to reinforce the trenchworks
which stretched towards the town. Scots were reported at
Nunraw, ready to take part in an assault on the 8th August
with Angus leading and the German auxiliaries forming the
first main thrust. A spy reported from Edinburgh that Mary,
Queen of Guise, had attended a funeral there the previous
day in which the corpse was dressed in hose and doublet
of crimson satin, with several chains of gold. The Queen
was said to be deeply moved, "wepying manye teares", so
speculation claimed the corpse to be Pedro Strozzi "for they
say the King would think a less loss of the whole army than
this one man". The walls of St Mary's were still standing

and the besiegers had fired into Haddington from the top of
the steeple, but were soon forced to leave by the cannons'
reply from the town walls. The church roof was in a sorry
state and the pillars supporting it badly battered. The town
cannons fired through the church continuously and "slew
six men at two shots on the far side of the church", together
with many of those engaged in digging trenches "so that the
French scant find men willing to work".
Brende also wrote to Paget on the same day, confirming that
the town was now under siege and trenchworks stretched
towards the walls. Indeed, only the thickness of the walls
separated English and French troops, a matter which was
resolved by a sturdy individual soldier inside the town who
was a maker of flails by trade. He fashioned a device which
incorporated a number of flails bound together, with a heavy
plummet of lead tied to the end and a stout truncheon at the
other which he could hold while he beat down on the enemy
below. In this fashion he slew and maimed a great many of
them and curbed their desire to approach too close to the
walls of the garrison.
French losses included three captains "whom they greatly
lament". The bulk of the Scots army was yet to arrive,
but Scots nobility were already present in some numbers,
including "the Earl of Argyll. moch contrarie to all mens

45

expectacion". Strong winds had forced the French fleet to ship anchor, but two had still run aground including one in pieces at Aberlady. Brende confirmed (inaccurately as it later transpired) that both old and young Queens and the Regent had sailed for France.

The following day, July 3rd, 1548, Palmer and Holcroft wrote to Somerset to report a French artillery barrage coming from Interaction 53 four or five cannon on the Lethington side which caused little damage "for they within make it up faster than those without beat it". A further assault was expected within five days "but we have good hope in our willing men..............to repulse a greater number by God's help".

Also enclosed was a letter from T. Gower to Brende describing the siting of the French cannon "in the little cornfield betwixt it (Clerkington) and Wyndham's bulwark with but two cannons as yet which began to shoot at ten o'clock this day. The cannon of Dunbar is come to Nunraw and shall be placed tonight at the mill of the bankside of the Friars to shoot into the town...........they are not laying any ordnance at the rock against Bowes' bulwark".

Argyll had arrived with only 60 men although others were expected. He was based at Lethington, the Regent's forces at the Nunraw with Angus nearby. Altogether 4000 Scots were in the field "of evill naghyt and lytell harnes and worse wepon for the most parte". They were well stocked with food supplies from Linlithgow and Stirlingshire. Eight galleys had arrived off Aberlady with ordnance to be landed. It was expected that the galley slaves would be forced to take part in an assault on the town. St Mary's still stood, with "a great band of foot behind it". Arquebusiers were firing into Haddington although the English reply took its toll "for Frenchmen go daily away in carts to be buried at Edinburgh and I take them to be gentlemen". He concluded with a lament for "50 horse who do not come".

On July 4th Palmer and Holcroft again reported to Somerset. This time it was about a French cannon which was broken.

English casualties included "Otterburn is sore hurt on the head and his servant slain at his heels" plus a master gunner
and eight more slain. It was claimed that D'Essé and the Scots Governor "with divers gallants" came to inspect a suspected breach in the defense walls but were fi red on from Wyndham's and Taylor's bulwarks. Four or fi ve of the party were killed "and bore away the legs of a dozen at least. For they say that our guns have that property to pick out the best of the herd". The Governor and D'Essé retired quickly, not satisfi ed that the information that they had received was correct. A spy had reported that a trench was being dug leading to Holcroft's curtain where cannon were to be brought to bear. A further 4000 reinforcements to the besieging army had arrived in Edinburgh and were expected to arrive the next day. Petro Strozzi had been injured but had recovered. French numbers were placed at 5000 foot and 500 horse, supported by 4000 Scots. Brende also wrote to Paget from Berwick confi rming the artillery barrage which had been going on for two days, but again claimed "ours repair in the night more than is done in the day". Supplies of powder, together with more men, were expected to be sent to Haddington within four days. The following day, July 5th, Palmer and Holcroft brought Somerset up to date with the news of Patro Strozzi "shot through the thigh by an arquebusier and carried in a cart by his men, in crimson and white velvet". He had advised the besiegers "to cease battery and make a small trench to the brink of the ditch, cast in earth and faggots to hinder the flank, and then assault round about, for he saw there not sufficient men to keep the walls". Accordingly trenches were dug towards Wyndham's and Bowes' bulwarks prior to a general assault, which so far had been deferred owing to the Scots refusal to take part. Some Germans had taken
up positions at the "Justice" with two cannon which had commenced fi ring on the town "but our men are all lodged

47

under the ramparts". The Queen had visited Hermiston to hold a Council for the marriage. The message ended with further promises to supply the Haddington garrison within the next few days. Obviously some reports from spies were incorrect, either deliberately on the part of counter-spies, or because rumour was confused with truth.

The following day saw a message from the same duo to Somerset describing an attack by the French the previous night at Wyndham's bulwark where they had been able to batter down the walls of a house, but they were repulsed and the walls repaired.

Brende wrote to Paget on this day to recount the presence of the Queen Dowager, plus sceptre, crown and sword "to be delivered to the Lieutenant of France". Preparations for attack were still ongoing. Relief was to be attempted on the morrow.

Matters became more serious for the garrison according to the letter Holcroft and Brende sent to Somerset on July 7th. "They have silenced our ordnance and so the matter remains to be tried at the point of the weapon ; many of our men are slain and, among others, Hennege, Tiberio and Pelham hurt". The French had cut off and undermined the point of Wyndham's bulwark. Yet hope remained, based mainly on the arrival of fresh reinforcements "110 of Wyndham's band, 150 of Gamboa under Petro Negro, of Bagshotte's band and volunteers of all sorts 100, including Your Grace's servant Chetwood..........they are all mounted arquebusiers, each with a bag of gunpowder and a roll of match before him". Lord Grey remained with 2000 foot "on this side the Pease".

THE ABBEY DECLARATION.

On this same day Mary of Guise attended a meeting of
the Scottish Parliament held at the Abbey of Haddington
convened by Arran and also attended by the French
Ambassador D'Oysel, in which the betrothal of Mary, Queen
of Scots to the French Dauphin was formally announced,
in return for considerable French aid in getting rid of the
English from Scotland.

Meanwhile, on July 9th, one James Henryson was writing a
long letter to Sir John Thynne and William Cecil in which he
described the breakdown in relations between England and
Scotland and set out the benefits of a permanent Union.

On July 11th an important letter was sent from the Privy
council to Shrewsbury instructing him to despatch 3/4000
men to Newcastle, and to remain on the Border as Lieutenant
until Lord Grey returned. He was advised that 2000 German
troops were at sea en route to join him, and that the following
Friday or Saturday would see Lord Clinton set sail from
Harwich with a strong force of ships and men.

Brende complained to Somerset on July 12th that he had
taken over the control of the work and pay of labourers at
the siege and sought the help of two clerks.

July 13th saw Palmer and Holcroft again warning Somerset
of imminent assault by the French who "have placed their
ordnance, ladders and faggots for the ditches". Nevertheless
the English raised a strong defence "there is no breach or
flank taken away. Their platform in the church is useless, the
town has so beaten the stones about their ears. Two pieces
on the Mount dismounted, their mine counter- mined, and
Interaction 57
a great mount raised that masters their bulwark, as they
outside may see..."

Details of a skirmish were revealed, in which a party from the
garrison, out collecting corn, were attacked by James Doig
with 100 horse, some foot and some Germans. Two of the
attackers were killed, one being Captain More, a lieutenant
officer "under the Rhinegrave" while more than sixty others

49

were wounded. The corn was safely collected. The French were all for retiring to Edinburgh but Arran persuaded them to stay for the assault saying "that all promised shall be performed and peradventure more". It was reported that the Queen, Mary of Guise, had gone to Dumbarton "to deliver the young Queen".

Palmer and Holcroft described the French tactics to Somerset in a letter dated July 14th -"they have now tried battery, mine and annoyance, and for famine they can have no hope, the Scots know the provision so well". Grey was expected to arrive with horsemen at camp at the Pease with foot to follow the next day.

The following day they were again in communication with Somerset describing a near assault by the French and Scots which was repulsed by the garrison batteries "so much shot fl ew out of the town that well was he that might turn back and hide his head". A French captain of foot, together with 70 or 80 men, were lost in the assault with many wounded. Arran and D'Essé were at loggerheads, the former lamenting the destruction of the surrounding countryside and giving his opinion that the town would never be taken, while D'Essé claimed it was the Scots lack of help in preparing trenchworks etc. which was hindering the assault. Evidently the Scots were so fed up that 1000 of them had given up and

gone home. The French said that they would await the arrival of the Highlanders and Argyll's men before commencing any attack.

Palmer was to go to Coldingham on the morrow to join Holcroft and some reinforcements.

TUESDAY'S CHASE.

Disaster struck on Tuesday, July 15th. According to Ulpian Fulwell, acting on information received that the Scots were leaving and the probability that the French would therefore go too, Grey sent a party of horse and foot, including Palmer, Holcroft and Brende, to a camp at the Pease. Palmer decided to ride back to Haddington to check the condition of the fortifi cations. At Linton, he was advised by the Captain of the troops protecting the bridge there, that there were enemy forces in the area. Palmer joined up with Sir John Ellerkar, with 400 horse, who were suddenly attacked by French cavalry. A fi erce engagement ensued in which the English were gradually achieving the upper hand, when French foot arrived on the scene in overwhelming numbers. The cry went up to retire but the inexperienced English force chose to fight on. Palmer was taken prisoner while Holcroft and Brende escaped to Haddington. A chase followed, lasting altogether for some eight miles which cost the English some seven to eight hundred captured or slain. Most of the English foot returned safely but those mounted were almost entirely lost. A full account was given by Brende and sent to Somerset on the !7th July.

Beaugué, who provided the French version, gave a detailed account of the battle. D'Essé had sent off twenty troops as an advanced picket, supported by the Earl of Cassils with

Interaction 59

fi fty light horse. At the same time d'Andelot advanced with his battalion. Count Rhinegrave took another route with his Germans, slightly to the left of the French foot in order to attack the English fl ank. There were also six fi eld pieces sited on his fl ank, ready to fi re at the fi rst sign of the enemy. Skirmishing took place with neither side taking the ascendancy. M d'Andelot took two hundred arquebusiers and pretended to retreat but suddenly turned about and delivered a ferocious volley at the pursuers, killing a great number. This manoeuvre accomplished, he withdrew to more convenient ground which he vigorously defended for upwards of quarter of an hour. Meanwhile d'Etauges, supported by the Laird of Duns' forces, charged and killed several of the Albanian mercenaries. The remainder of d'Andelot's troops assaulted the English who were being kept at bay by the arquebusiers, which again resulted in much slaughter. All the while the French artillery was fi ring and killing large numbers of the enemy who nevertheless gave one last furious charge. Finally D'Essé, Lord Hume the Laird of Duns and M. D'Etauges led an attack on the English fl ank and carried all before them. Rhinegrave's Germans fell upon the retreating English at a crossroads causing them to fl ee. In this battle, it was claimed that the English had about 800 men killed and more than 2000 made prisoner.

Nevertheless, two days later Shrewsbury was writing to Somerset to tell him that he had arrived in Haddington with 5000 men "the rest to follow, as I have signifi ed". He ended with a plea for money to pay the newly arrived force. On July 22nd Wilford, the garrison Commandant, was advising Grey not to attempt any further engagement with the enemy

"for the town is fi ve times stronger than when they came. We want nothing but powder, shot and working tools". He added to this letter the following day, advising Grey to despatch supplies by horseback at night as well as seeking further information on Grey's plans.

On the 24th, Brende was lamenting the loss of so many in " Tuesday's Chase -"....of 300 demilances but 36 fi t for service, of 450 new light horse, not 100". He also complained about the West March horse (from the Border country). "Many come from Court with letters to have pay at Lord Grey's discretion, having neither horse nor harness, then get pay and do no service ; 40 of them consume the pay of 300".

On July 30th, Thomas Fisher wrote to Somerset advising him that the "assured" Scots had made up the loss in horse, according to Lord Grey. Orders had been issued that same morning to reinforce the Haddington garrison with powder, shot etc.. which was to be delivered by John Carr's command. 38 men of war had sailed past St Abb's Head heading north, being due in the Forth on the next tide.

CLINTON.

August 6th saw Shrewsbury and Grey asking Admiral Clinton to sail further up the Forth to drive the French fl eet away, for "wanting these the army cannot advance and the enemy shall not retire". There was also the presence of twenty "victuallers" to the French fl eet which Clinton would miss if he instead sailed for the Tay. Their instructions were explicit -"When in the Firth of Forth employ yourself by landing on the Fife side, and make as if to land at Leith, also fortifying at Burntisland, if you and the engineer think

Interaction 61

it requisite ; if so, say how soon it may be done, to what purpose and of what strength, and if the ships may lie there at low water ?"

Next day, Grey was advising Somerset that, in response to requests from Wilford for more powder, lead, match and arquebuses, some had already been despatched some ten days previously, but, being seen en route, the land convoy had taken shelter at Lauder, until a more convenient moment arrived. Grey wrote in similar vein to Wilford on the 10th, advising him to save as much powder etc.. as possible until new supplies arrived, and that the reason for the delay was due to "waiting for our horsemen".

Clinton replied to Shrewsbury and Grey (probably on the 9th) saying that, as his fl eet approached Leith, about 40 ships and galleys fl ed, "some to Inchcolm and some to Burntisland, where landed 500 men and burned twelve ships and galleys, all full fraught with victuals, wine, bread, biscuit, fi sh and butter and one with cider". Six ships, from 140 to 300 tons, were carrying cannon. The garrison of 500 fl ed leaving Clinton with fi ve sailors as prisoners. They told Clinton that Leith was under fortifi cation, Petro Strozzi being the designer "who is daily borne about in a chair with four men. 300 Scots pioneers are at work, plenty of victuals and some great artillery (part broken) is laid in the great church there".

Clinton said he would lie off Leith and keep the enemy occupied as requested.

August 14th saw Shrewsbury and Grey reassurring Wilford that help was on its way albeit they were waiting until the

Scots had gone, reportedly in eight days time, at which time
the French would be on their own. However if Wilford felt
that he could not wait until then, they promised to set forth
sooner.

Grey also wrote to Somerset, advising that the town's troops
had been successful on two occasions ; fi rstly, in an attack
which had captured thirty to forty horses and carriages from
the Highlanders and secondly, by fi ring a cannon into the
Abbey killing four men. Reports were coming in that the
French fl eet had advanced further into the Forth, to take
wounded on board. Between 500 and 600 men were being
sent to strengthen the garrison at Dunbar.

On the 16th August Brende sent Somerset a full muster of
foot in Scotland (see Appendix C) totalling some 11,412
plus another 1300 still at sea with Clinton. He promised to
send on the number of horse when he had completed the
muster. He estimated them at 1800.

A further report to Somerset, from Shrewsbury and Grey
on the 18th August, reported Clinton's action in burning
Kinghorn, Kirkcaldy and other towns in Fife. A rumoured
assault by the French on Haddington, due for the next day,
was deemed unlikely to take place because the Scots were
not ready. A skirmish near Lauder was reported in which Sir
John Ellerkar had captured ten to twelve of the enemy and
slain six for the loss of fi ve or six.

Grey again asked to be relieved of his command. so that he
could go home to his family.

On the 18th August Clinton sailed from Berwick with a
fl eet of thirty men-of-war at the same time as Shrewsbury
marched with 12,000 foot and horse, arriving at Spittal Hill
near Longniddry on the 23rd. D'Essé appealed to Arran for
the 6000 Scots he had promised but the Queen intervened
and a decision could not be reached in time to stop the relief
force entering Haddington on the 24th August, 1548.
D'Essé was forced to retreat to Musselburgh, the siege

temporarily over. He set an ambush using "a little hill not far from the town" for concealment and was able to drive the English back to Haddington having suffered the loss, it was claimed, of 300 slain and/or captured. Not long after the French decamped and returned to Edinburgh. D'Essé now set about fortifying Leith, to such an extent that many left Scots left Haddington, Dundee, St Andrews, Stirling and Glasgow to set up house there, Leith being regarded as a safer option in the current warlike time.

CAMISADO.

On the 10th October, 1548, D'Essé having returned to Musselburgh with a well rested force of men, delivered a secret but determined night attack, or "camisado", on the Haddington garrison. French troops succeeded in breaking a port, having fi rst surprised and overpowered the Italian guards and then advancing along a narrow lane into Haddington town itself. The guards they encountered were all put to the sword and some English soldiers killed in their beds, all at little or no cost to the invaders. D'Essé kept his troops close to him in one body as they crept slowly forward along the passage which was fenced in with trenches and earthworks. De Beaugué claimed that of 500 who rose to the defence of the town some 250 were slain without a single attacker having fallen, but, given that the action took place in a narrow passage and did not occupy much time, this claim is probably exaggerated. Nevertheless success seemed fi nally to have arrived within the grasp of the attackers, but, at the crucial moment, fate intervened in

the shape of a French deserter, or "renegado", who ran to a cannon which was placed between two gabions (wicker baskets filled with earth in the narrowest part of the lane. He fired at point blank range, and the ball burst through the massed, closed ranks of the invaders, causing a massive slaughter as well as alerting the garrison. Confusion, fear and doubt at once spread through the French ranks and they began to retreat, hotly pursued by the now thoroughly roused garrison. Although all credit is due to the "renegado" who saved the day, nevertheless it is unlikely that the cannon was placed in such an ideal spot by accident, nor that the passage just happened to be conveniently narrow. Although De Beaugué gives it as "a ball that made its way through our massed ranks" it was more likely grapeshot and chain. D'Essé now considered his options back in the French camp. Having narrowly failed to take Haddington and heeding the advice of his commanders who doubted if it would ever fall, he turned his attention to the other strongholds , including St Andrews, St Johnstone, Aberdeen, Montrose and Blackness.

The number of French troops in Scotland at this moment in the campaign decreased considerably, with many returning to France after their tour of duty, some killed in battle and several falling victim to the onset of plague. To remedy this loss four companies of foot set sail from Bordeaux and, after enduring a long and stormy voyage, eventually reached Dumbarton.

SIEGE CONDITIONS.

All the while conditions within the town of Haddington deteriorated steadily albeit there were periods when relief was
Interaction 65
to hand, notably when Shrewsbury arrived with provisions, ammunition and troops, and earlier when Wyndham and Adam Selinger made a courageous sortie and brought in between two and three hundred fresh troops and life-saving victuals. Thereafter it was a matter of hair-raising dashes to Dunbar, where the town was under English occupation although the Castle was held by the French, plus occasional sorties by the garrison as reported by De Beaugué -"........ the Governor himself broke out upon the head of 400 English and Italian foot and 60 Scots peasants with a view to seize upon some barley..............nigh the Fosse. Twas in autumn".

Shortly after, though, Wilford was writing to Somerset "..... the state of this town pities me both to see and to write it,

but writing to Your Grace I hope for relief. Many are sick
and a great number dead, most of the plague. On my faith
there are not here this day of foot, horse and Italians 1000
able to go to the walls, and more like to be sick than the sick
to mend, for they watch every fifth night, yet the walls are
not manned, they lie in litter without beds, go in their single
white coats, for there is small provision of clothing..............
the houses are so beaten, they lie in "cabens" (cabins ?) .....
the corn in the store like to be spoilt in foul weather..........
great lack of labourers and all things".

His mood was slightly more optimistic, though, in his letter
of the 11th November to Somerset. "I shall get as much
corn as I can and put it in meal as I have casks for...........
and for victuals, if the country remain unspoiled, it can well
furnish them.............I have got 18,000 fish for this town and
I think I can get more...."

His optimism appears not to be justified, for Fulwell reports
that over the next two months ".....our enemies did so beat
the town with shot that they left not one whole house for our
men to put their heads in, whereby they were constrained to
lie under the walls" and "........the scarcity of victuals among
them was so great that they were constrained to eat horses,
dogs, cats and rats........these extremities....made them look
more like ugly monsters than human men".

THE CIVILIAN POPULATION.

Although no precise figures are known it is certain that
the civilian population of Haddington did not entirely
flee when the English forces occupied the town. We have
already seen a reference to "....60 Scots peasants who made
a sortie from the town to sieze barley". Wilford also refers
to ".......two Scotsmen burgesses of this town, who have
served very honestly during the siege, and have suffered
great losses..........one of them is George Forresse, brother
to Davy Forresse, the other John Rickenton is his cousin
German........"

This is a reference to a George Forrest who appears in the

Haddington Council records on October 8th, 1544, nearly four years before the siege, as a member of the Council Court. He also appears on December 6th, 1545 ...."Which day George Forrest announced that an Act had previously been passed by the Provost, Bailies and Council, in which it was stated that all manner of persons who were still unclean or suspected of having the plague, should leave the town within eighteen hours, under penalty of death and confi scation of goods". In view of what was to happen in Haddington some three years later it must have grieved the same George that this course of action was not available to
a stricken populace.

It would seem therefore, that some burgesses and councillors were prepared to stay while the siege took place until the situation became totally impossible. Nevertheless all was not lost, for, on March 17th, 1551, eighteen months after the siege had ended when order was restored and the town was in full fl ow again ".........the Council ordered tenant farmers to pay Robert Maitland the sum of eight merks for keeping safe the documents of the Burgh of Haddington........."

Chapter 5

RESOLUTION.

The loss of Wilford was felt very acutely among the Haddington garrison. Some wanted to advance on Dunbar Castle straightaway to rescue him but wiser counsel held that would leave Haddington dangerously exposed. Nevertheless his reputation was such that morale in the troops was very low for a good while.

James Wilford was the eldest son of Thomas Wilford of Hartridge, Kent, by his fi rst wife, Elizabeth. The family came from Devonshire. His grandfather was Sheriff of London in 1499 and his great-uncle Edmund was Provost of Oriel College, Oxford between 1507 and 1516. James was brought up as a soldier's son and fought in the war in France in 1544-5. In September 1547 he was appointed Provost-

Marshall of the English army and took a leading part in the Battle of Pinkie for which he was knighted at Roxburgh on the 28th September. The following saw James promoted to Captain and charged with guarding Lauder Castle. He served under William, Lord Grey de Wilton, at the capture of Haddington, and was recommended by him to become the Governor of that town. On the 3rd of June he captured Dalkeith, then returned to Haddington.

For once De Beaugué and Fulwell agreed that Wilford was the man for the job.........."a man of great diligence" and "apt for that charge". De Beaugué refers to "..........the great reputation which the Governor had deservedly acquired". Fulwell referred to him as "the Flower of Fame" and declared " Wilford was one such as was able to make of a cowardly beast a courageous man" and "He was so noble a captain that he won the hearts of all soldiers. He was, in the

town among soldiers and friends, a gentle lamb. In the fi eld among his enemies, a lion. To his men benefi cial. To all men liberal". Brende, writing to Paget, said "..........the Captain has pretermitted (forgotten) nothing, and is wonderfully esteemed and beloved of all".

Wilford, meanwhile, was unwell, suffering from a sword slash to the head. He was sent as a prisoner to Stirling Castle from Edinburgh. An exchange was arranged in November 1549, and Wilford arrived in York, "very weak", on the 21st of that month. He retired from the army and, on the second of February, 1550 he was granted the Manor of Otford in Kent. Still suffering from his wounds he died there in November 1550.

THE FRENCH CAMPAIGN ELSEWHERE.

His counterpart, D'Essé, meanwhile was of a mind to alter his tactics. The defenders of Haddington had proved surprisingly obdurate and seemingly resistant to direct attack. He resolved, therefore, to keep them under siege while he directed a large part of his forces to other parts of Scotland and England where the English could be

more easily attacked and removed from the fi eld. After
consultations with the Scottish commanders he decided to
march to Jedburgh, in Tweeddale, where English sympathies
were widespread, to "prevent the English from fortifying
and securing the footing they had got in that country".
His campaign took in successful attacks on Ferniehill
Castle and Cornhill Castle, after which the French troops
under D'Etauges set about laying waste the countryside
between Jedburgh and Newcastle. D'Essé, confronted with
the problem of feeding his troops in a desolate landscape,
Resolution 71
and with an English army marching towards him, retired
to Melrose and thence to Leith. There then followed a
successful assault on the English garrison on Inchkeith
island in the Forth, undertaken at the express wish of Mary
of Guise.
The Earl of Arran had twice tried to capture Gray Castle,
using a force of 8000 men together with eight pieces of
cannon, but had failed. On the fi rst occasion his troops
were suddenly needed elsewhere, and on the second the
Earl of Argyle had negotiated a truce with the Governor of
the Castle, which had bought suffi cient time to enable an
English force to arrive and raise the siege. Having done so,
they then built a new castle at Broughty nearby, from which
they were able to send between 1600 and 1700 lancers and
foot soldiers to occupy Dundee, encountering no opposition
worthy of the name. D'Essé was stung into action. He
sent Count Rhinegrave with two companies of German
mercenaries and D'Etauges with one company while he
himself followed as quickly as he could with the remainder
of the forces he could spare from the siege.
The English, alerted to this advance of the enemy, set fi re
to Dundee and retired to their two fortifi cations nearby at
Broughty. When D'Essé arrived he set to fortifying Dundee
with seven companies of French troops plus two of Scots,
supported with cannon and ammunition, before he himself

returned to Edinburgh. His remaining troops were winterquartered
at St Andrews, St Johnstone, Aberdeen, Montrose and Blackness.

Meanwhile Lord Hume had determined to retrieve his own Fast Castle from the English occupiers who had been in possession since the Battle of Pinkie in 1547. The Castle

stood on a rock commanding the high road between England and Scotland. Access was diffi cult. Nevertheless a night assault was attempted. A sentinel spotted someone climbing a wall and raised the alarm but, when the Governor of the Castle arrived he saw nothing and, because it was such a dark and stormy night he derided the sentinel saying no one would assault the Castle in such foul weather. This allowed the Scots lying in wait to climb over the walls unobserved and kill the unfortunate sentry. Thereafter the Castle was swiftly taken.

D'Essé reluctantly decided that he had probably achieved all that he was likely to achieve in Scotland. After so long an absence he sailed back to France in a galley, taking with him De Beaugué among others.

His replacement De Termes had already landed at Dumbarton with 100 men-at-arms, 1000 foot and 200 light horse. Meanwhile Wilford's replacement was Sir James Acroft who took over the command of the Haddington garrison, remaining there for the best part of a year. As we have seen, De Beaugué had returned homewards and so was unable to provide an account of further events relating to the siege. Even Fulwell confi nes himself to a remark that during the time that Acroft was in command "many noble acts were achieved". What is certain is that the besieged continued to endure the most appalling privations brought about by hunger, plague, lack of shelter and bad weather. Brende, writing to Sir John Madson on November 29th, 1548 says "..........the country is so wasted that there is nothing to destroy...........the bareness, want of lodging, scarcity, wet

and cold, makes war here more painful than elsewhere".
Things did not improve in 1549. But by far the worst element
in a growing nightmare was plague.

PLAGUE.

Plague is caused by a bacterium, Yersina Pestis, which can
infect rodents. It is usually transferred to humans by fl eas.
Plague was everywhere, it seemed, respecting neither friend
nor foe. Thomas Fisher wrote to William Cecil on September
17th, 1549 saying "I feared at fi rst I had been infected by
the plague, which reigneth extremely from Northallerton
northwards in every village and not one house clear of it
in all this part of Scotland and Berwick". Civil authorities
were equally at a loss as how to cope. Houses, suspected of
infection, were often sealed off, but there were no houses
left standing in Haddington. Ports were kept fi rmly shut
against any visitors, and this of course was certainly the
case during the siege but still the plague wreaked havoc.
When Wilford wrote of having barely 1000 men left to man
the walls, then half of the garrison, at least, must have been
infected. No measure, however extreme, including burning
all possessions belonging to those even suspected of being
a carrier, proved effective. Having to huddle together for
shelter and warmth in the corners of collapsed buildings
or damp cellars only exacerbated the problem. Nothing it
appeared was to be done except to endure. The only relief
from plague was due, although unknown to anyone, to the
evacuation of the town by rats because there was not enough
food left to eat. Forays continued to be made to secure
some supplies, and attacks on the fringes of the besieging
forces provided some relief from the intense boredom and
frustration the surviving English troops must have felt. For
the most part, it was a case of fi nding some hole to crawl into
for shelter, wrapped in whatever clothing they still owned.

SOMERSET.

Back in London, Somerset was confronted by a rapidly

deteriorating situation, both at home and abroad. His over-ambitious pursuit of the Protestant faith had caused widespread discontent in England. Coupled with a worsening of general economic conditions in the country was a feeling that he had served his own self-interest too well. It all resulted in a series of uprisings which, although put down with some severity, still left a residue of simmering resentment among his enemies, especially the Earl of Warwick who was determined to remove the Protectorship from Somerset. On the 8th of August, 1549 war was declared on France, whose forces were already besieging Boulogne. More particularly the Scots, aided by the French, had recaptured all of the castles and strongholds held in Scotland by the English with the exception of Lauder and Haddington. The infant Mary, who was supposed to be the intended bride of Somerset's ward, Edward, had instead landed in France and was destined to marry the Dauphin. The carefully planned strategy, designed to unite England and Scotland, lay in pieces. Somerset decided it was time to cut his losses. Reports were coming in that the French and the Scots were assembling an even larger force outside Haddington with a view to attempting another assault, while the exhausted garrison were doubtful of their ability to resist for much longer. In September, 1549, Somerset sent word to the Earl of Rutland, stationed at Berwick, to march on Haddington and withdraw the garrison. No sooner had he sent this message than on the 14th of October Warwick

Resolution 75

and the Council of England indicted him on charges of abusing his power and sent him to the Tower. He made a full confession and was released as a free man on the 15th of February, 1550, having been stripped of the Protectorship. However his freedom was short-lived because, a year later on the 16th February, 1551, he was arrested on a charge of plotting to kill Warwick and take the Crown for himself. These charges were not successful but a further charge of felony was . On January, 1552. Somerset was beheaded.

ARRAN

His old adversary, Arran on the other hand, was doing rather
well. He had made a fortunate decision in backing the French,
especially Mary of Guise and the plan to marry off the infant
Mary to the French Dauphin. His reward, the Dukedom of
Chatelhérault, came in 1549. He had not forgotten that as
great-grandson to James II he was heir-presumptive to the
Scottish throne, which claim Mary of Guise acknowledged
should her daughter die childless. In return she took over
the Regency. However the Dauphin was to become King of
Scotland, following a secret agreement, which was a severe
blow to Arran. He took little persuading to change sides
when the Lords of the Congregation agreed to support his
candidature if Mary, now Queen of Scots, could be removed.
Arran was opposed to Mary's marriage to Darnley but the
rebel forces he led against her were defeated, causing him to
fl ee to France in 1565. He returned to support Mary, this time,
upon her return from exile only to be imprisoned by Moray in
1569. After signing the Pacifi cation of Perth in 1572, naming
James VI as successor to Mary, he retired from public life
and died in his bed in 1575.

76 Resolution

MARY OF GUISE.

Mary of Guise, as shrewd as ever, was determined to build
on what had turned out to be a successful campaign. The
English were in retreat and her daughter was safely in
France, betrothed to the Dauphin. She herself sailed there,
landing at Havre on 19th September, 1549. She set to work
immediately, seeking support for an Irish uprising against
the English occupier to be reinforced by the French. In this
event she was destined to fail, but switched her attention
back to Scotland where she was more successful on her
return in persuading Arran to surrender the Governorship
to her once her daughter had reached the age of twelve.
For the next ten years she was involved in a struggle with
the religious reforming bodies, especially John Knox who
was always ferociously opposed to her and her advocacy of

Catholicism. She died peacefully on 11th June, 1560.
HADDINGTON.
Haddington itself, of course, suffered dreadfully. Not a
house was left intact because the French and Scots gunners,
frustrated in their attempts to break through the earth mounds
which surrounded Haddington, had determined that at least
no safe hiding would be available in any house. The original
shape of the town was a long, isosceles triangle with the base
of the triangle running parallel to the river Tyne. Each leg
of the triangle was composed of houses, mostly two storeys
tall, some built of stone, some of wattle and straw. All were
now in ruins. Only rubble was left following the ferocious
barrage of the cannons beyond the walls. As Fulwell wrote
"........our enemies did so beat the town with shot that they
left not one whole house for our men to put their heads in,
whereby they were constrained to lie under the walls, for
other lodging was there none." In dry weather, men could
just about manage to get about the town, but in winter when
the rain and snow fell, the conditions underfoot almost
defi ed description.
St Mary's still stands, as it has since 1139, but the effects of
the siege were calamitous, causing great destruction. Only
the nave survived ; the tower, transepts and choir were left
entirely roofl ess. Indeed the walls of the church bear the
only remaining visible evidence of the intense fi ghting that
took place, in the shape of holes and gouges that cannon
and arquebus fi re caused. John Knox intervened in 1561 to
persuade the Town Council to repair the Church "frae steeple
to the west end". Over the centuries further improvements
were made but it was not until as late as the 1970's that
the fi nal and greatest restoration was carried out. Today the
church stands proudly by the riverside, intact and secure.
Just how intense was the fi ghting which the church endured
is illustrated by the contents of a letter from Thomas
Palmer to Somerset on July 2nd, 1548 "The walls of the
church yet stand, and the enemy has shot with "cutthrottes"

into Haddington from the top of the steeple, but the town ordnance made him leave it. The "vawltes" of the steeple and church were broken, the church uncovered, the pillars cut and under propped, thinking they might have turned it over when they had list, but they have failed, and we think it shall do no hurt, for our ordnance beats through the steeple at every shot........"

The target was the Scots and French troops who cowered to the rear of the church and listened to the shot whistling by.

78 Resolution

THE AULD ALLIANCE.

The alliance between the two groups was still an uneasy one. The Scots were not a united force, many of them still in shock after the Battle of Pinkie, many of them still with friends and relatives within the town walls, and nearly all of them deeply suspicious of their new-found friends from over the sea. The French were no less doubtful about their allies who did not appear to act as wholeheartedly in the common cause as might have been wished. As De Beaugué observed "........all the Scots, excepting 600 lancers that depended upon the Earls of Arran and Huntly, withdrew to their respective homes. And here I take it, twill not be improper to observe by the way, that the Scots never take to the fi eld but when forced to arms by necessity". Palmer, writing to Somerset on July 15th, 1548, observed "Thus the two (D'Essé and Arran) contended, and the Scots so weary of it that 1000 stole from the fi eld this morning". Finally and much more seriously from the Alliance's point of view, while D'Essé was encamped in Edinburgh, a riot broke out. De Beaugué recounts "........the Scots and French were living together in perfect unity and friendship when one of the French, an unknown inconsiderable fellow, had some ill words with two or three of the citizens, and from words they proceeded to blows. Upon this, a great many Scots run to the hurry, and were carrying the Frenchman to prison, when on the other hand some Frenchmen made haste to rescue him. This had liked to have proved a most scandalous error and

to have been followed by most pernicious consequences,
but the officers were not at all to be blamed, for they no
sooner heard of the quarrel than they put an end to it with
equal haste, difficulty and danger. Which done they instantly
Resolution 79
delivered up the author of the sedition and he was that same
day hanged in the Grassmarket of Edinburgh".

This incident served as a salutary lesson to both camps,
and spurred D'Essé to decisive action against the English
in order to prove to his Scots allies that the French meant
business.

CASUALTIES.

Casualties on either side are impossible to quantify with
any degree of certainty. Fulwell and De Beaugué favoured
their own when it came to making any estimate of those
killed in combat. Both agree that " Tuesday's Chase" was
disastrous to the English, with 800 slain or captured, but
as for the other conflicts the estimates for those killed
differs widely between the two authors. Despatches from
Palmer to Somerset spoke of "............sixteen carts full of
dead" and "French dead carried off hourly in carts" while
Holcroft admitted "............many of our men are slain........"
In the "camisado" or night attack of October 10th, 1548,
Fulwell claimed five hundred of the French were killed,
but De Beaugué refutes that figure claiming that it was the
English who suffered the most casualties. From despatches
generally, the impression is formed, however, that it was the
plague that was the most voracious killer, and this was surely
more likely to have affected the tightly- confined English
garrison more than the besieging forces who, at least, were
able to move camp should the occasion warrant it.

So far as the rank and file soldiery was concerned, the
fate of the individual goes unrecorded. No memorial was
ever erected to the dead. As for the officers on the French
side, D'Essé, d'Andelot, d'Oisel, Peter Strozzi and Count
80 Resolution
Rhinegrave survived to return home. D'Etauges was

captured, de Biron was killed at the landing on Inchkeith island, while Captain Jalinques died of fever. Villeneuve was killed at the siege. On the English side, Wilford and Palmer were both captured but later ransomed, the Master Gunner (name unknown) was killed and Hennege, Tiberio and Pelham wounded. The others, presumably, survived.
THE FINAL RELIEF.

At Somerset's command, despite early reluctance on the part of those he instructed, Henry Manners, the Earl of Rutland, who had replaced a totally exhausted Grey de Wilton in May 1548, set forth from Berwick in late September 1549, with six thousand men. The French and Scots watched them in silence as they advanced to Haddington, but did nothing to intervene.

On the fi rst day of October, the remnants of the garrison were gathered together, the town was set alight and razed to the ground while reliever and relieved walked out, never to return.

Some walked, some were carried, some travelled in carts and wagons while a few officers rode on horseback. From one of the wagons, which carried pikes, muskets, arquebuses, bows etc.. there dangled a fl ail, its metal ends bloodstained. The enemy watched them go, in turn taking their time to enter the town which they did a few days later, once the fl ames had subsided. Mary of Guise remarked "........the enemy have left nothing behind them but the plague".
The bedraggled convoy of men dragged its weary way, for the most part silently, until with a great shout of relief, they came at last to Berwick.

Chapter 6

CONCLUSION.

When the townsfolk returned to Haddington to start rebuilding their ruined homes, the late protagonists were engaged in new struggles at different venues. The leaders of the respective armies in the siege took a different view regarding the overall outcome. Somerset realised that his strategy had failed, in fact it was all over on the day that the young Mary sailed from Dumbarton for France and her Dauphin. Failure represented a rich opportunity for his enemies at court to join forces against him, an opportunity they were quick to seize.

On the other hand Arran was quick to seize the momentum of the moment and turn it to his advantage. It was not long before all the English had been sent packing -Lauder Castle being the last to give up the struggle. Would that it had been as easy to dispose of his enemies at home ! For the time being however, Arran could reflect on a successful campaign. His personal standing though, did not seem to have increased in stature at all. Scotland was still not united, and no faction looked to Arran as the future leader of the country.

Mary of Guise, shrewd as ever, continued to thwart Arran at every turn, looking for her big chance to take over the Governorship, which eventually did come to her. Meanwhile her daughter was safely ensconced in the French court, learning a new language, a new way of life, and preparing to take on her role as wife to the Dauphin. The bigger prize of the Scots throne lay some time further ahead. For Mary of Guise, things were going very much according to plan.

The respective commanders of the forces in the field could take little comfort at the outcome. Wilford was a prisoner of the Scots, although shortly to be exchanged. His standing as a leader, however was enhanced by his conduct during the siege. His troops adored him for his attention to their needs in a difficult situation and for his undoubted courage in always being at the forefront of battle. He was unlucky to be denied the rewards such behaviour would surely have brought - promotion and a career in the military service of his country which may well have brought him the highest honours.

For D'Essé, his counterpart on the French side, the siege of Haddington revealed surprisingly weak aspects to his abilities as a commander. Although De Beaugué was unstinting in his praise for his commander, nevertheless a more objective view shows several opportunities which were not taken up, opportunities which could have turned the tide. Firstly, the reduction of the southwest bastion surely invited D'Essé to storm it and sieze control before going on to enter the town itself. No attempt was made to do so, leaving even De Beaugué puzzled and leading to an accusation of timorous behaviour on the part of the French leader.

Secondly, the initial success achieved by the surprise "camisado" was not developed as quickly or in as much strength as it should have been. D'Essé's forces outnumbered the English by more than two to one, and probably at that moment by even more because of the effects of the plague, but there was no attempt to fl ood the breach with soldiery. When the considerable numbers which the Scots were able to bring to the fi eld are added, it can be seen that the odds against the besieged garrison were overwhelming, but D'Essé was never able to launch a coordinated attack on the ramparts. At one stage, 8000 Scots and 6000 French, including mercenaries, were ranged against a maximum of 2,500 English, even assuming the latter were all fi t. A more adventurous and determined commander should surely have been able to mount a combined assault, one which might well have brought the garrison to the point of surrender. Such an attack could and should have been preceded by a heavy mortar bombardment. Cannon fi re quickly proved to be useless, but D'Essé had many years of experience of siege warfare, so it is a considerable mystery why no mortars were brought to bear on the besieged garrison. All too readily, it appears, D'Essé gave up on Haddington and, with a sense of relief, turned his attentions elsewhere. If there were any who deserved to be called "Heroes" it can only have been those soldiers who withstood eighteen months of siege life, enduring on the way, the worst of weather, continual shortages of food, powder, shot and other supplies, who very quickly did not even have a room with a bed to lie on, who instead lay out in the cold wrapped in

rapidly deteriorating clothing, but who were always ready
to turn to arms at the first sign of danger. Afterwards, they
must have wondered if it had all been worthwhile, even
though at the time they gave no thought to why they were
there, but merely "stood to" when called.

Fulwell was so moved by their plight and by their spirited
defence that he composed a poem in their honour :
"A commendation of the English soldiers that served at this
Siege of Haddington".

The frowning, furious Dame,
That high Bellona fierce,
That grieving goddess whose outrage
Doth kings and countries pierce,
Drew forth her bloody blade,
Set up her standard black,
And fenced with her fiery flag
To work her wrathful revenge.
Now who can leave scotfree then
That dares abide the tumult ?
The noble heart for honour fights,
The Tyrant hunts for spoil,
The coward cringes for words
And hopes for happy day.
Yet is he not the first that strikes
Nor last that runs away.
At point of hard distress
A hardy man is known.
At rattling shot or hunger sharp
A dastard is down thrown.
But when Bellona saw
The warlike English wights
That at this siege in martial acts
Displayed their whole delights.

BIBLIOGRAPHY.
- L'Histoire de la Guerre d'Ecossse ; pendant les campagnes
1548- 49 -Jean de Beaugué -ed.J.Bain (Maitland Club 1830).
- The Rough Wooings -Marcus Merriman (Tuckwell Press 2000).
- Histoire d'une capitaine boubonnais au XVI siècle : Jacques de
la Brosse, 1485-1562 ; ses missions en Ecosse. -ed. G.Dickinson
1929 (SHS 1942).
- Calendar of the State Papers relating to Scotland and Mary
Queen of Scots 1547-1603 ed. J.Bain 14 Vols.
(Edinburgh 1898).
- The Flower of Fame (1575) -Ulpian Fulwell -reprinted in the
Harleian Miscellany, ix, 368-374, ed. T.Park (1808-13).
- A Short History of Haddington - Grey W.F. and Jamieson J.H.
(Edinburgh 1944).
- Haddington -a Royal Burgh -a history and guide
(East Linton 1997).
- The Early Maps of Scotland 1524-1548 -Inglis HRG etc.
(Edinburgh 1936).
- Mary of Guise - Marshall R.K. (1977).
- The Lamp of Lothian, or the History of Haddington, in
connection with the public affairs of East Lothian and Scotland-
Miller J (Haddington 1844).
- The Battle of Pinkie, 10 Sept 1547 - Oman CWC (Archaelogical
Journal XC, 1-25, 1934).
- The Anglo-Scots Wars, 1513-1550 -Philips, Gervase
(Woodbridge 1999)
- Somerset and Scotland - Pollard AF, EHR XIII (1898) 464-472.
Dictionary of National Biography -Stephen L and Lee S (eds) -
63 Vols.
- Royal Commission on Ancient and Historical Monuments of
Scotland Inventory (1924).
- Henry's VIII's Army -Paul Cornish and Angus McBride -Osprey
Publishing (1987).
- The Betrothal of Mary, Queen of Scots -Tudor and Valois
Politique in Scotland 1543-1544 (Tuckwell Publishing 1996-7).

APPENDIX A

French offi cers at the siege of Haddington.

Andre de Montalambert, Sieur d'Essé -Lieutenant-General of the army in Scotland.

Lord d'Etauges -in charge of the cavalry.

M d'Andelot -in charge of the foot soldiery.

Count Rhinegrave -in charge of the German mercenaries.

Lord Peter Strozzi.

Captains - Loup

Beauchatel

Longue

de la Chapelle de Biron

Villeneuve

Achaut

de la Maillereye d,Oisel

Gourdes

Lucenet

Gaillard

Argenlieu

d'Ouartis

Jalinques.

APPENDIX B

English officers at the siege of Haddington

Sir James Wilford -in command of the Garrison

Sir Thomas Palmer -engineer and artichect of the fortifi cations

Sir Thomas Selinger

Sir Oswald Wolftrap

Sir Robert Morsley

Sir James Acroft

Captains - Pelham

Dethick

Wood

Wyndham

Taylor

Tolbie

Fitzwilliam

Whitten

Booth

Pikeman

Cam

Carton

Bagehot

Ashley

Lawton

Henneger

Bowes

Tiberio -in charge of the Italian mercenaries.

and later

Brende

Holcroft

Lords Shrewsbury and Rutland came to Haddington with relief forces.

88 Appendix C

APPENDIX C

"The numbers of men to enter Scotland with their leaders, 1548".

For the battle :

Thomas Sutton ; Sir Thomas Cokaine ; Robert Blont ; William
Nedeham ; Humfrey Stafford ; John Persall ; John Dodde
; Richard Morton ; Robert Savell ; Sir Francis Hastings
200 ; Sir Robert Constable ; Richard Tempest ; Sir Thomas
Malvery ; Sir William Vavasour ; Sir William Calverley ; Sir
John Nevill ; Sir Marmaduke Constable ; Francis Norton ;
Edmond Norton ; Thomas Beaumont ; John Lassey ; Hugh
Lassey ; Marmaduke Thwaites ; Sir William Saint Quintin
; John Gascoigne ; Robert Constable ; Sir Gervase Clifton
; Sir Anthony Nevell ; Sir James Fuliambe ; Martin Aune
; Sir Andrew Corbett ; Sir Anthony Mannering ; Thomas
Leigh ; Thomas Newport.
"The Forward" :
The Lord Latimer 200 ; Sir Thomas Holcroft 350 ; Sir
Richard Townley ; Sir Robert Langley ; Sir Laurence Smyth
; John Booth ; Thomas Barton ; Sir Thomas Holt ; Edward
Holt ; WilliamMyles ; Edward Sutton ; Sir Ralph Coppinger
200 ; Henry Gerard ; John Collins ; Henry Wilcox ; Sir
William Davenport ; Randall Mannering ; Sir John Leigh
;John Bavington ; John Baker 200 ; Edmond Tweedie ;
Colbie ; Sir Richard Sherborne ; Thomas Catherall ; Thomas
Churnoke.
For the "Rearward" :

Appendix C

The Lord Scrupe 200 ; Edward Horsley ; Lord Conyers 200 ; Percival Selby ; Lancelot Alford ; Sir Thomas Danby ; John Vavasour ; Sir William Fairfax ; The Lord Nevell ; Christopher Metcalf ; William Wycliffe ; Christopher Wyvell ; Robert Conyers ; Richard Stranguish ; Thomas Watterton ; Richard Wentworth ; John Vincent ; John Brown ; Thomas Craythorn ; George Soulby ; Thomas Holford ; Humfry Nevell ; Edmond Leigh ; Edward Blount ; " Spaniards 242".

Total 2842.

The Almaynes (Germans) battle 2020, of these 600 hackbutters.

Sum of all the footsoldiers - 11,412. Besides 1300 sent by sea.

I shall send Your Grace the number of horsemen as soon as I have mustered them. Besides this new supply from Northumberland, they amount to 1800 horse.

The 12th August, 1548

Signed : John Brende. (From a letter to Somerset).

N.B. Each leader had 100 men. Those with more are specifi ed. To assist administration, armies were divided into three "wards" along mediaeval lines i.e. the Vanguard (Forward), Battle and Rearguard (Rearward).

APPENDIX D
CHRONOLOGY OF EVENTS DURING THE SIEGE OF HADDINGTON.

1548

April 18th - Grey enters Haddington with 2000 foot and 500 horse.

June 1st -Fortifi cations almost completed. Grey leaves Haddington in the charge of Wilford.

June 30th -French army arrives. Siege begins in earnest.

July 1st to 4th -French digging trenches against the western and southern defences.

July 4th -Argyle arrives with the Scots army.

July 5th -Massive artillery bombardment.

July 7th -Treaty signed in Abbey. Grey sets out from Berwick with relieving force.

July 14th -Concerted French attack beaten off.

July 17th -" Tuesday's Chase".

July 18th - Mary of Guise visits Haddington and is fi red on.

July 22nd - Wilford describes Haddington as "fi ve times more impregnable".

August 18th - Clinton and fleet sail from Berwick.

August 24th -Relief force enters Haddington.

October (early) - D'Essé and French army retire to winter quarters in Edinburgh.

October 10th -"Camisado" -(night attack) -French repulsed with difficulty.

November (first week) - Wilford complains that the garrison is reduced to less than a thousand by the effects of plague.

1549

January - Wilford is captured at Dunbar. Sir Richard Acroft assumes command at Haddington.

August -English troops "at their last gasp". Proposal to evacuate the garrison.

September 14th -Earl of Rutland, with 6000 men, reaches Haddington. Garrison is evacuated to Berwick.

September 20th -Scots/French enter Haddington.

92 Appendix E

APPENDIX E
TRANSLATION OF ABBEY DECLARATION.
THE BETROTHAL OF MARY, QUEEN OF SCOTS.
Act of Parliament of Scotland, at Haddington, 7th July, 1548.

In the Parliament of Our Most Excellent Mary, Queen of Scots held at the Abbey of Haddington the seventh day of July the year of God one thousand fi ve hundred forty eight years by our noble and mighty Prince James Earl of Arran Lord Hamilton & etc. and Governor of the Realm the three Estates of the Realm being present.

Which day Monsieur D'Essé Lieutenant General of the navy and army sent by the most Christian King of France having regard to the ancient long confederation and friendship standing between the Realm of France and this country and of the mortal wars cruelties depredations and intolerable injuries done by our old enemies of England against our Sovereign lady being of so tender age her Realm and lieges thereof their several sorrows. Wherefore the said most Christian King being moved through the fraternal and confederation foresaid could do no less to aid support maintain and defend at his power this tender princess her Realm and lieges as a well-intentioned and helpful brother, contrary to all others that would attempt injury against the same, not by words but by way of deed and to that effect has presently sent him to this Realm with his navy and army of Noble men with such directions as to put this Realm to the old state of liberty privilege and freedom and to recover

all strengths Castles and Fortresses out of our old enemies' hands with the advice counsel and assistance of the Lord Governor and Nobles of this Realm to the best of their ability and to wage their own lives to that effect and not only has sent this army presently but also promises in his said master's name at all necessary times in the future to send and have in garrison men of war munitions and money in this Realm in such quantity that shall repress our said

old enemies the English during the time of war and keep
and defend this Realm from them and all others in liberty
and freedom conforming to his commission obligation
and promise given to him under the said most Christian
King's Great Seal shown and produced before Parliament.
Therefore having consideration of the promises and how
that the said most Christian King has set his whole heart
and mind for the defence of this Realm desires in his said
master's name for the more perfect union and indissoluble
brand of perpetual friendship love and confederation the
marriage of our Sovereign Lady to the effect that the said
most Christian King's eldest son and Dauphin of France
may be joined in matrimony with Her Grace to the perpetual
honour pleasure and profi t of both the realms observing
and keeping this Realm and the lieges thereof in the same
freedom liberty and laws as has been the casein all the time
past of all of the Kings of Scotland and shall maintain and
defend this Realm and the lieges of thesame as he does the
Realm of France and the lieges thereof conforming to his
commission promise and direction as produced previously.
And therefore desires my Lord Governor and three Estates
of Parliament to come forward and give their decision as to
whether the aforesaid wish be reasonable and acceptable
or not. The Queen's grace (Mary of Guise Lorraine) our
Sovereign Lady's most dear mother being present my Lord

Governor and three Estates of Parliament as previously
mentioned all in one voice have found discerned and with
the consent of Parliament concluded that the wish of the said
Monsieur D'Essé Lieutenant in the name of the said most
Christian King his master (Henri Cleutin, Sieur D'Oysel his
Ambassador present in the said Parliament confi rming the
same) to be very reasonable and have granted that our said
Sovereign Lady be married with the said Dauphin at her
coming-of-age and presently give their concert thereto. So
may the said King of France keep maintain and defend this
Realm and lieges of the same, the liberty and Laws thereof as

he does his own Realm of France and lieges of the same. And just as this Realm has been kept maintained and defended by the Noble Kings of Scotland in times past the same will be kept by the promise of the said Lieutenant special commissioner in the said cause and that our Sovereign Lady be married to no other person but the said Dauphin alone. My Lord Governor in our Sovereign Lady's name ratifi es and approves in this present Parliament the decision and consent of the three Estates of the same being present concerning the marriage of our Sovereign Lady with the Dauphin of France conforming to the Act of Parliament made thereupon. Providing always that the King of France, the said Dauphin's dearest Father, keep and defend this Realm, its lieges and Laws as they have been kept by every king in times past in Scotland and to marry her to no other person but the said Dauphin alone".

Published in : Acts of Parliaments of Scotland, 12 Vols, (ed) T.thomson & C.Innes, Edinburgh (18144-1875), Vol.", pp 481-2.

Index

96 Index

The Siege Of Haddington
by
Gerald Urwin
Price £9.99

32064556R00049

Made in the USA
Charleston, SC
07 August 2014